THE LAUGHTER GOES FROM LIFE

THE LAUGHTER GOES FROM LIFE

In the Trenches of the First World War

Thomas Penrose Marks

WILLIAM KIMBER · LONDON

First published in 1977 by
WILLIAM KIMBER & CO. LIMITED
Godolphin House, 22a Queen Anne's Gate,
London, SW1H 9AE

ISBN 0 7183 0055 6

Photoset by Input Typesetting Ltd., London
and printed in Great Britain by
The Pitman Press, Bath.

Contents

A map of the area covered appears on page 23

To my wife, Barbara,
without whose encouragement this book
would not have been written

Preface

This book is not intended as a recrimination of our 'enemies'. The purpose of it is to make clear the fact that we have no 'enemies' as such. For friendships formed, and for acts of chivalry and kindness performed by those on both sides of 'No-man's-land' we are grateful. These are things which are worthy of him who is little lower than the angels.

Perhaps the most valuable legacy of the war – if we are able to appreciate it – is the knowledge that battles do not end a quarrel. They merely intensify it and perpetuate it. The soldier at the Front learnt to discount the policy of hate. Though he did not love his 'enemy', he did not hate him.

A new generation has arisen which knows not war. There is danger in ignorance, as in forgetfulness. And men should not forget that fundamentally, civilised peoples are not vastly unlike, They all have something to contribute to life.

Half of a long lifetime has passed since this book was written in 1936, but the manuscript has lain in a cupboard for forty years, and only recently come to light again.

Another war has been fought, with the Germans again the aggressors. Perhaps Sir Winston Churchill was not far wide of the mark when he said of them that they are always either at your throat or at your heels.

Centuries from now men will read of the first use of poison gas, liquid fire, concentration camps, torture chambers, the destruction of a hundred fair cities, the mass murder of millions of ordinary men and women, and all the other diabolical crimes which were committed during two World Wars by the nation which has also produced so many just and famous men. It is indeed a sorry record.

I have been back to the Western Front in peace time, and motored along the four hundred miles from the Belgian coast to Switzerland. In some places the trenches may still be seen, but by and large the work of restoration has gone ahead, and the countryside has taken on its normal appearance. But every few miles one sees military cemeteries, some of which are the last resting places of thousands of warriors, like the vast one at Passchendaele. They are well looked after. And all along the old battle line most impressive monuments have arisen, such as that on Vimy Ridge to the Canadian troops.

At Polygon Wood where many brave Australians fell, including my wife's eldest brother who was just over 19, the caretaker of the cemetery told us that remains of fallen soldiers are often found. Pheasants emerged from the trees which surround the cemetery. Many headstones of unknown warriors bear the simple inscription, 'Known Only Unto God'.

At the Menin Gate my wife and I heard the Last Post sounded by a bugler at 6 p.m. one evening. It rings out all over the Salient at this time every evening, and all the traffic through the gate comes to a halt for several minutes.

About thirty miles to the south we came upon a discarded 18-pounder field gun. It was beside 'Westminster Bridge', and tall grass and weeds grew there. A mile away at Givenchy, a French woman showed us two soldiers' helmets – one German and one British – which she had dug up in her rose garden. A German trench had run across the garden. Beside the road at this point was a memorial to the 55th British Division which had greatly distinguished itself there, and repelled a ferocious German attack. On the memorial we read these words, 'They win or die who wear the rose of Lancaster'.

Right across Belgium and France we saw where many millions of men had fought each other for over four years, and where several millions had laid down their lives in the 'war to end all wars'.

CHAPTER ONE

Nip Goes Under

The country around us is bleak and desolate in the extreme. As far as the eye can see there is nothing but mud. The ground is everywhere pock-marked with deep shell-holes. In places they overlap. They are all full of the filthiest water and mud.

Our Battalion is in the line in the Poelcapelle sector a few miles to the north of Ypres. The Salient is acknowledged to be the worst part of the Western Front. There is no cover anywhere, and there is no certainty of being relieved when the time is up. Our home is on the edge of a shell-hole. If we slip we get wet. If we slip far enough we may even disappear by falling into the water and mud. When we are shelled, we slide as far as possible down the side of the shell-hole and hang on. There is nothing else to do.

There is a slope ahead of us. The enemy is better off than we are. His positions are higher than ours, and so he can look down upon us. Jerry always seems to be in possession of the high ground along every part of the Front. He chooses carefully and well, and hangs on grimly to every vantage point.

We dare not move in the day-time. Only at night may we get out and stretch ourselves. We long for darkness to come; the cramp becomes unbearable at times.

In this sector, the rule is two days and two nights in the front line. The journey to the rear is a nightmare. We would almost prefer to double the time in the line and to halve the number of journeys.

There are no communication trenches, so we go over the top. There is always a guide, but no man can guide others in these parts. It is necessary to stick to the duck-board tracks or be irretrievably lost. These tracks are not wide, and they are not straight. They are laid across the shell-holes so that you can walk in reasonable comfort. They are just like ladders with the cross-pieces close together.

The worst of these duck-board tracks is that they are just as visible to the enemy as they are to us. He knows exactly where they lie, and his guns have the exact range. That is why you never know if the relieving troops will arrive on time.

Every night these tracks are shelled heavily. If you are on your way up to the front line, or if you are going to the rear, you chance your luck. It is impossible to time your journey. One night is never the same as the previous night. Sometimes nothing happens for hours, and the relief takes place without incident.

It may take nearly all night to move a mile in these parts. If you get off the track, you sink into the mud and can hardly move. You can scarcely put one foot in front of the other. You add pounds to your weight if you walk a dozen yards.

One night, two of us were told to carry hot soup to the forward positions. My companion was the smallest man in the Company. In civilian life he had done all kinds of jobs. Before enlisting he had been a collier; before that, he had worked in a baker's shop. Life had never been easy for him. Only with difficulty could he sign his name. His face was wizened; though very young, he was very wrinkled. One could think of him standing at a street corner or outside a pub on a Saturday night, with cap pulled well down and a thick scarf knotted round his neck. His blue eyes were small and keen and kindly; his nose was too long; his smile was attractive, but he looked destined for tragedy. There was a great deal that was good in him. He swore much, and often, but always in a nice way. He was clean in thought, and there was not an ounce of vice in him. He was the only man I have ever seen who carried two water bottles. One of them contained rum. He never drank his rum ration, though he always received it. It was kept in his bottle and was given to anyone who looked in need of it.

He never bought any cigarettes or tobacco, but he always took them when they were issued. He smoked only one cigarette a day. Two draws and a spit was one of his rules of life. In between times, he chewed a little cut plug. The remainder of his cigarettes he gave away to the heaviest smokers when they wanted a smoke more than anything else. He would keep them waiting as though he enjoyed the feeling of largesse. We called him 'Nip'. This may have been a diminutive of 'nipper' or small person. Everybody liked him, although he always seemed to be in the way of someone. When they swore at him, he took it good-naturedly.

The hot soup was put into a large metal container. When full, it was about the maximum weight a man could carry. It was carried on his back. One side of it was concave. A piece of sackcloth covered it. Straps passed over the shoulders and under the arms. In a few minutes the metal became hot, and one could feel it burning one's back.

We had half a mile to go, and we took turns in carrying it. When you had gone a hundred yards, the heat became unbearable. We carried each other's rifle when not carrying the soup container. It was dark, and we could not see the duck-board.

Nip walked on ahead; he said he knew the direction fairly well. We had scarcely gone half-way when he came to grief. The track bent round to the right, and Nip walked straight on. He fell into a shell-hole of the filthiest mud and water imaginable. He sank inches each minute; the soup and container weighed him down. Only by his yells could one tell his position. I lay down on the track and stretched out a rifle. He managed to grasp it, and gradually threw off the soup container. It sank gurgling into the mud. It may still be there! The ever-alert Fritz heard the row and plastered the area with high-explosives.

With a tremendous mutual effort, Nip emerged from the shell-hole. He was soaked to the skin, and his teeth chattered. When he reported what had happened, he got no sympathy. He was called all the names under the sun. The Army has an extensive vocabulary, and particularly when it is hungry and fed-up and far from home.

When we go back on rest, we have miles to walk. The only people we ever see are soldiers. They live in all kinds of places. Everybody looks for cover. A few planks or old pieces of zinc are invaluable. They help to keep out the rain. They deflect the bitterly cold winds; they screen you from a watchful enemy. In these parts they are of more value than many rubies. It is curious what constitutes value. Before the war, the peasants used these things for any odd purpose. Now, they preserve life. Things are not always used for what they were intended.

We move back through the ancient town of Ypres. In mediaeval times men came from many lands to buy and sell here. The skill of the Flemish weavers was displayed in the hugh Cloth Hall. Now it has been destroyed. Only a few feet of the stone walls remain. Another link with the past has been broken. Man's inventions have destoyed man's handiwork. Nothing is permanent.

One does not linger long in the streets. The long-range guns drop shells into them every day. The transport wagons hurry forwards and backwards, and men live under huge piles of débris. They crouch to go through their doorways, just as Eskimos do when entering their igloos.

Our tramp, tramp, sounds hollow as we go along. We seem to be passing through a ghost city as we move along the cobbled roads. There are no civilians to be seen here. Their homes have been destroyed, and all have fled westwards.

Our rest billets are only tents and the camp is nearly a foot deep in mud. On moonlight nights enemy aeroplanes come over. They drop bombs upon the camp, both on the forward journey and on the return trip. It is a terrifying experience. You are impotent. If you stay in the tent you cannot do anything. If you move out of it, you are no better off. Most of us stay where we are, and hope that nothing will come our way. You hear the roar of the engines above you, and you sometimes see the planes if they come sufficiently low. You hear the swish of the falling bomb. Then comes the ghastly explosion, followed by the cries of the wounded.

Each time we come back on rest, there is a bathing parade. We move off by platoons to the Divisional baths. They are in a field about a mile away. There are many large tubs in the field, and each is about a third full of warm water.

We hand in our clothes to the man in charge. Our uniforms are disinfected while we wait. We change our underclothes for others which have been de-loused. We do not know who has worn them before, and it is useless to ask; no one knows. We hop into any tub that we can find. Three men to a tub is the usual number. If none is available, we wait until a man jumps out. He dresses where he stands. At first, one is shy of doing these things in public; but since it has to be done, one soon ceases to be modest about it. If you are late, the others soon begin to swear at you for keeping them waiting. We all move off together.

For a day or two we expect to feel a little more comfortable. But it cannot be for long. The ground itself, and everything we have to touch, seems to bring forth vermin. Nothing keeps them away. We have tried all kinds of insecticides, and some of us carry spare vests and shirts. But it is all to no purpose. We are all as lousy as coots. We itch all over, and scratch ourselves until we bleed. It is of no use.

We are glad to return to the line again. The rest billets are no better. There is, in fact, more work to be done when you are out of the trenches than when you are in them. Every night carrying and digging parties are required. It is often an all-night job, and when you arrive back at the camp in the early morning, you are exhausted.

When in the front line, you want to be out of it, and when out of it, you often wish to be back again. We are like fish out of water wherever we go and whatever we do. This might be explained by saying that the soldier is never contented. But it would probably be nearer the truth to say that it is the ego which is in a perpetual state of rebellion. The desire for change is really the desire for safety. Most nervous people complain of anxiety. Life at the Front destroys our nerves. There is danger about us, and below us, and above us. It is always present, and never at any time very far away from us. We know that we are not as steady as we used to be. Those who are not for us, are against us, and life has become very circumscribed.

We can never wander at will, and our horizon is a very limited one. At times we cannot even gaze above our shell-hole. When in the trenches, we walk six paces to the right, and then six paces to the left. It is as bad as suffering solitary confinement in a prison.

We become introspective, and begin to think and to try to reason things out. When you do that kind of thing, you are lost. Then one becomes dissatisfied with oneself, and this does not help matters at all. Age always has one advantage over youth. Experience must always be bought. But the price may be too high.

We live in a state of expectant dread. We have become apprehensive, and we have to repress our feelings and our emotions. This objective-anxiety is really our ego expressing itself. An instinct is manifesting itself. The ego is always busy attempting a flight. No sublimation is possible. We wish to get far away from it all, but our conscious mind decides that our wish cannot be realised. The unconscious psyche censor is at work trying to repress our wish.

This is the reason why we shall become nervous wrecks in time. A year at the Front is enough for any man, and more than enough for most men. After that, we become too highly-strung.

When we leave the line, and go back for a short rest to Siege Camp, Dirty Bucket Camp, or to the hutted camp at Kempton Park near Langemarck, the German airmen often make the nights hideous by bombing us. For good measure they also shower down, frequently, masses of little sharpened steel rods several inches long and as thick as a man's forefinger. Being dropped from such a height, they can go right through a person.

A new edict has gone forth already. We expected as much, so it does not come as a complete surprise. A raid will be made upon the enemy posts each time the Battalion is in the front line. The news is not welcome. The reason for this order is that the enemy's morale may be severely shaken if we raid his front line posts often and keep him jittery. We do not doubt that the raids succeed in accomplishing this aim. But neither have we any doubts about the effects of raids by us on our own morale. There are few things that are more disastrous.

A reconnoitring patrol is sent out during the night. It consists of a second lieutenant and three men. The three men are badly wounded, and the lieutenant manages to get back in safety to our lines.

The remainder of the night is spent in bringing in the wounded men upon stretchers. They cry out as we stumble in the darkness. We cannot help wondering how much nearer is the end of the war as the result of the work of the reconnoitring patrol. The one thing of which we are sure is that there are three men fewer for tomorrow.

The next time in the line, another raid is carried out. The raiding party consists of two second-lieutenants and about thirty men. At ten o'clock, covered by an artillery barrage, they 'went over'. Three prisoners were captured.

The nett gain on the two nights' work is nil. Each side has lost three men. Numbers are curious things; they tell all kinds of stories. It is difficult to say definitely with whom the advantage lies. In a football match, three goals each would be called a draw, no matter if one side spent three-quarters of the ninety minutes of play in the territory of the other side. Perhaps the rules of the game are different when all those who take part are classified as cannon fodder.

The following day a German is wounded by a corporal. He tries to get back to his lines, but accurate rifle fire keeps him pinned to his shell-hole. Every time there is any sign of movement, a rifle cracks out. Then all becomes quiet again. A careful watch is being kept upon him. We know that he is still there, because we can hear him shouting at intervals.

At night, soon after darkness falls, a party goes out to bring him in. He is too weak to offer any resistance, even if he wished to do so. Now he knows that he will be well cared for, and is quite satisfied to see the rest of the war out in captivity. Our hospital authorities will care for him, and not feed him on rye bread and sauerkraut.

We are leaving the concrete fortresses and pill boxes; the duckboard tracks and the water and mud-filled shell-holes; the decomposing corpses of men and mules, and all the desolation and misery of the Salient. And we hope never to return here.

CHAPTER TWO

We Live Like Lords

We seem to have come into another world. Our Battalion is at Beuvry, about twenty miles south of Ypres. It is only a hamlet, and we are comfortably billeted in an outbuilding on a farm. There is plenty of straw available and we sleep warmly at night, although we lie on a cement floor. It is lovely country, this part of France, and we would be happy to remain here for the duration of the war.

In our squad there is a butcher and a baker. It is not often that you get this combination out of a dozen men. There are many who would like to join us. They they will have to wait until our number is reduced by illness or casualties, unless they have some special contribution to make. At present, we are sufficient unto ourselves.

I am the youngest of them all, and am lucky to have been taken on by them. We stick together and do what we can to help each other. No one of our party is over forty, and there is only one other under thirty. I do all the buying for the squad because I can understand the French language and make myself intelligible to the shop-keepers, housewives and others. One other job which I do is to write the letters home for three of our members.

The acknowledged leader of our squad is the most experienced man. He has never worked in his life. That is sufficient qualification. In civilian life he is a professional burglar. He does not hesitate to tell us about his adventures. Though he cannot write, and can only read with great difficulty, he is an excellent raconteur, and has a delicious sense of humour. He is big and upstanding, and keeps us interested by the hour.

Our second-in-command is a big raw-boned Scot. He came south from Glasgow many years ago, and has lived most of his life in London. He is cautious and very shrewd. He has never volunteered for a night patrol or a bombing raid.

Another of our members worked in a chocolate factory in Bristol. He is a thoroughly decent fellow, and rather timid. His chief value to us is that his firm continues to send him a box of chocolates each month. His younger brother works in the same factory, and also sends out what the firm allows him to take home each month.

The butcher, the baker and Nip are numbers five, six and seven. We have also a brick-layer's assistant, a clerk, a university student and a horse-trainer. I have only just left school, and have not yet begun to take life seriously.

Before the war, none of us knew the others. But here we quickly sort ourselves out. Being thrown together, we soon find that there are other things in life besides the nature of our work. There is nothing to keep us apart, and we become almost indispensable to one another.

After spending only a couple of days at Beuvry, we have moved to the fairly large town of Bethune. It is within gunshot range of the Front, but it has not been badly knocked about. Most of the inhabitants are still in the town.

We are in a big yard which has only one entrance. There are large gates opening on to the street. Surrounding us there are tall buildings. One of them is a brewery, and several brewer's drays are still in the yard. The stables are nearby.

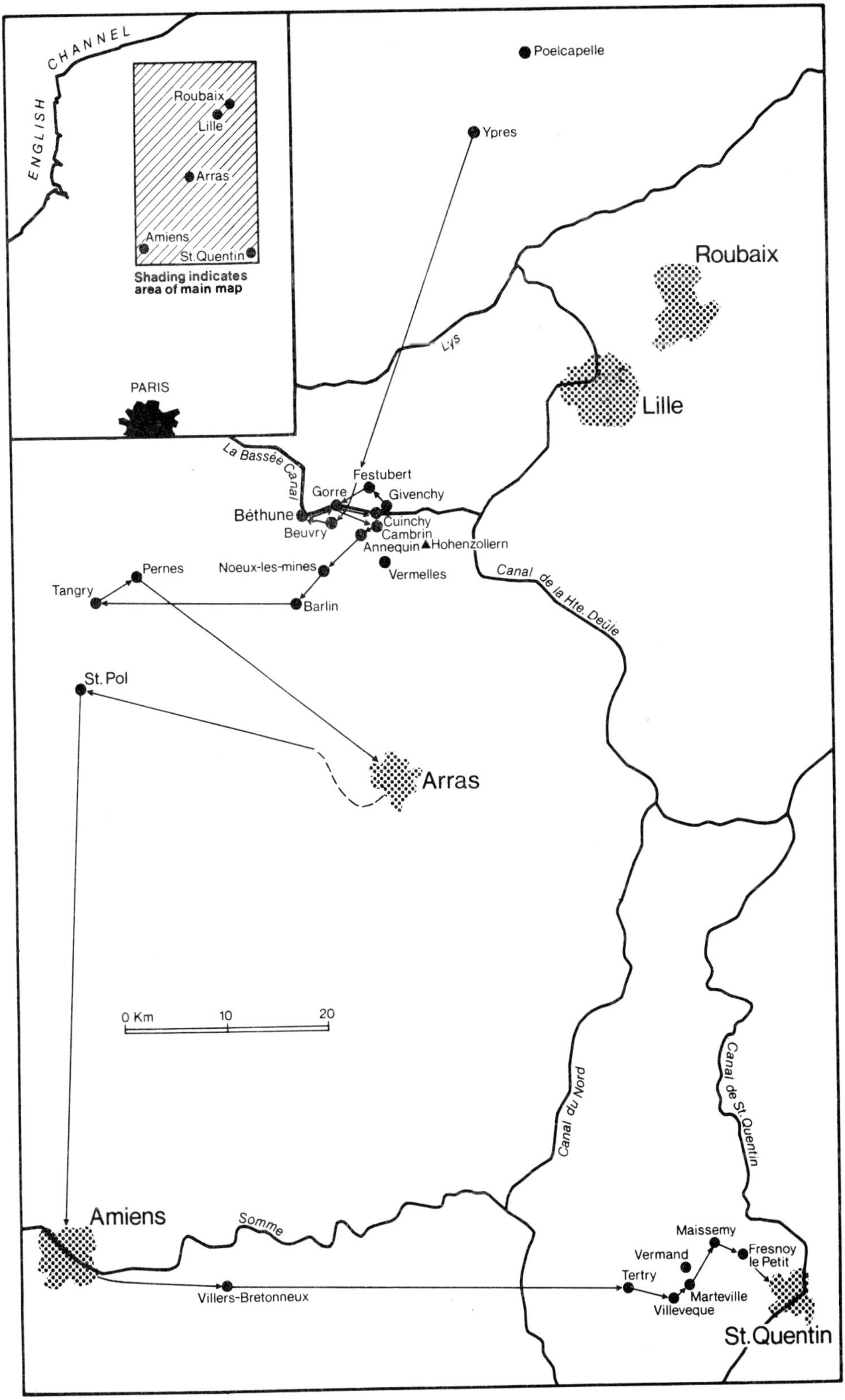

ENGLISH CHANNEL
Roubaix
Lille
Arras
Amiens
St.Quentin
Shading indicates area of main map
PARIS
Poelcapelle
Ypres
Roubaix
Lys
Lille
La Bassée Canal
Festubert
Gorre
Givenchy
Béthune
Cuinchy
Beuvry
Cambrin
Annequin
Hohenzollern
Noeux-les-mines
Vermelles
Pernes
Tangry
Barlin
Canal de la Hte. Deûle
St. Pol
Arras
0 Km
10
20
Canal du Nord
Canal de St. Quentin
Amiens
Somme
Maissemy
Vermand
Fresnoy le Petit
Tertry
Marteville
Villers-Bretonneux
Villeveque
St.Quentin

One wall collapses as a shell hits it. The masonry falls chiefly on our field kitchen. We were just about to have our dinner, and some men have already drawn their portions. It was our turn for roast meat and potatoes, but the cooks have served up stew, followed by rice and raisins boiled together.

A second and then a third shell follow the first. We can scarcely see across the yard; it is so full of dust. It gets into our eyes and noses and mouths. We cough and spit. Because the yard is surrounded by tall buildings, the noise is intensified. Bricks fall everywhere, and fragments whiz past us. The enemy has the exact range of the place, and it would be suicidal to stay here. The shells come over in salvos. We count them – one, two, three, four. There must be one battery trained on to the spot where we are. The brewery is built of red bricks and is a tall building.

We cannot see the gate-way, but we know where it is, and we do not wait after the second salvo comes over. Before the third is due, there is a scramble towards the open gate. We push our way out into the street and go to the right and then to the left. We run for a quarter of a mile until we see a house that stands in its own grounds. We think that it will be less conspicuous than the houses in the middle of the town, and we go into it.

It is unoccupied. The owners have already fled. While coming along, we saw many civilians hurrying down the street. They were leaving their homes for the second time. A few of them carried goods in their arms and on their backs. Others pushed wheelbarrows, hand-carts and perambulators hastily laden with what was deemed of value. There were mothers with their babies in arms, and small boys and girls ran beside them. They all looked terror-stricken, and seemed scarcely to know which way to go. It would be many miles to the next town where they would seek a roof over their heads, or stay with friends or relations.

One woman was wounded as we passed along the street. Eight soldiers rushed to help her. They carried her on an old door to the nearest doctor. We could not do anything for her.

A wall of the house we are in has been half-destroyed, but this does not worry us. Perhaps it was just a chance shot that damaged it. If so, another will not come our way. We decide to make our home here. We could not possibly be better suited. The remainder of the Battalion is a long way off, and we shall not be bothered much with fatigue parties. Those who are nearest to headquarters will have to turn out more often. The orderly sergeant will not want to come so far to search for us.

The twelvc of us settle in as though we have known the place all our lives. Two bedrooms are in good order, and the sitting-room can soon be cleaned up. There is a good deal of rubble in it, and some of the furniture has been broken. But we do not mind that.

We throw down our equipment and our rifles as though we have finished with them for ever. Then we proceed to make ourselves at home. If the owners return we shall gladly give up the place to them. If they do not come back, we intend to stay here until the Battalion has to move elsewhere.

Looting is strictly forbidden. It is a military crime which is punishable by death. We have heard of actual cases that have happened. We act within the law as far as possible, and it would be difficult to bring a case against us. We destroy all the possible evidence, and do not carry anything on our persons. We do not seek to enrich ourselves at the expense of the townspeople who have left their homes. But the term 'looting' is capable of a wide interpretation. If you find a bottle of wine and drink it, you are guilty of looting. If you catch a fowl that crosses your path, and kill and eat it, you are guilty of looting. The plain fact of the matter is that every soldier on active service has, at some time or another, laid himself open to the charge of looting. Clearly, it would not be possible to punish everybody, so the practice is to make an occasional descent upon someone, and make an example of him.

We sleep four in a room. Those in the bedrooms are better off than they have ever been in their lives. They sleep two in a bed. When you look for them, you can hardly find them. They have feather mattresses, and they just sink into them. There are plenty of blankets, and many spare ones in the cupboard. We have four each. We do not need so many, but this, for us, is the height of luxury, and we decide to enjoy it to the full.

Two of the beds are four-posters, with a canopy over the top. They are heavy and very old. The woodwork gleams in the candle-light. Most of us have two pillows each. Those who could only find one put a cushion underneath to give the extra height. It is the first time we have seen linen for many months. I sleep on a sofa in the sitting-room. It is long and well-sprung. It is covered with green plush. As I lie upon it, I think that some craftsman derived pleasure from making it, and the owner looked after it well.

We take it in turns to walk down to the cook-house to draw rations for twelve men. But we only do this for the sake of appearances. We do not intend to use the rations. We keep only the bread. The remainder we give away as we come up the street. We have no use for tinned beef and cheese and hard biscuits. We even sacrifice the tea. We intend to live like lords for a few days, and enjoy life to the full while the going is good now that we have really fallen upon our feet.

If we did not draw our rations, somebody would notice it. We do not want anybody to start making enquiries; it might be inconvenient to us. It would cause endless trouble, and perhaps we should have to share what we have found. If the Company Officer knew what we were doing, his servant would just be sent to transfer the goods from our kitchen to his own.

We seem almost to have come into an hotel. The house is full of provisions. It looks as though the inhabitants expected the war to last for ever. There is no shortage of anything. There are scores of tins of beef and salmon, and twenty-nine tins of jam. We do not even look at the beef and jam. We have had these things every day for many months and long for a change of diet.

They are two-pound tins of jam. The labels indicate apricot and plum-and-apple. But we know that they are not true to type. They contain a large percentage of turnip tops. Someone has made a fortune and gained a knighthood. And the plum-and-apple jam doubtless came from some quartermaster's stores when the French troops were withdrawn and our own took over this part of the Front.

The civilian people buy these things from the British soldiers. One can always raise some ready cash by selling them. Cheeses, too, are in great demand. Many quartermaster sergeants have grown almost rich in this trade. Rum always fetches a good price, and it is so very easy to carry. A water-bottle full of it will fetch twenty francs anywhere. Fresh meat, too, is a valuable commodity. Our ration of it is never very large. A pound a day is the regulation issue, but we have not had a pound in a week. If you find two lumps of it in your soup, you know that somebody else has not got any. You could put both pieces into one egg-cup.

It is no use complaining. The rations are made-up at the Base, and at every depot between the Base and the Front somebody has a dip. There is a break-of-bulk at the Headquarters of the Army Corps, Division, Brigade, Battalion and Company.

From time to time one is found out carrying a sand-bag into civilians' houses. But the risk is not great, if the business is properly organised, and it is possible to become well-to-do. Many have chosen this way to enrich themselves. It is an old soldiers' practice. The many must go short for the benefit of the few. In the past, we have even gone over the top at night in search of tins of beef. In times of plenty, they are thrown away. When the rations have not come up, we have even eaten the contents of tins which have been half rusted through. Jerry thinks that we live well. He is a great meat eater, and prizes our bully-beef highly.

But now we live on the fat of the land. There is plenty of flour and sugar and eggs. A side of bacon hangs in the pantry. In the garden there are plenty of potatoes and carrots. There was also a young sucking pig. The butcher tied a rope to its leg and led it away. We thought that everybody would hear it squealing. In an hour's time he returned; the job was skilfully done.

The first night we had roast sucking-pig. There was crackling too. We had almost forgotten about such things. Each of us had three helpings. There were roast potatoes as well; as many as we could eat. Afterwards there was rice pudding. Then the baker came to light with jam tarts, both big and small. We washed them down with coffee – white and black. The cellar contained many kinds of wine unknown to us, as well as the cheaper varieties which we had often bought at the estaminets.

There is plenty of wood and we have a large fire. It burns all day and we sit round it in the mornings and drink coffee and smoke cigarettes. When the coffee pot is emptied, we fill it again. The demand is great.

There are no parades, and we feel that we belong to the leisured class of society. In the afternoons we rest, and take it in turns to make the coffee. Those on duty carry it to the others. We drink it as we lie down, and do not think of moving until six in the evening. Then we come to life again. It is time to prepare the evening meal. We all help with the menial tasks. The butcher and the baker are in command, and they delegate our duties to us. We scrape the potatoes and boil the water.

The next night we have fried sausages and mashed potatoes. This is followed by boiled jam pudding. It is the first time that most of us have had it for years. After supper, we make up the fire. We sit around it and drink our coffee. The baker excels himself with cheese straws, and a large dishful quickly disappears.

This is the kind of soldiering that we really like. We hope that they have forgotten all about us. We could easily last out the war in these billets. We all agree that such a piece of good fortune may never come our way again, no matter how long the war may last, and decide to make the most of it. Then we cut for partners and play cards until far into the night. The twelve of us make three tables exactly.

At first, we play several rubbers of bridge. Our glasses stand beside us on the table. It is the business of the non-playing members to keep them filled. Before we finish for the night we play vingt-et-un, or, to give it the soldier's appellation, 'pontoon'.

Once each day a lance-corporal visits us. It is necessary for them to know where we are to be found, should we have to move off at short notice. We treat the lance-corporal liberally when his is on his rounds. It must take him a long time to complete them, as he probably stops for refreshment at every house which he visits.

After three days, we move off by Companies. It is too near to the line for a whole Battalion to march off as a unit, so we go off at half-hour intervals. All day we march back. There is a halt of ten minutes every hour, and an hour at mid-day. We unharness ourselves, and stretch flat out upon the ground to give our shoulders a rest. The straps have cut into them.

By the time evening comes, we reach our destination. We have covered many miles, and have arrived at the edge of a large wood. It has not been touched by shell-fire. There are squirrels living in the trees, and birds of all kinds fly from branch to branch. In the distance we hear the sound of woodpeckers. They are of two kinds.

There are no billets in the wood or near it. Perhaps no troops have been here before. We live in the wood and make bivouacs for ourselves with our waterproof sheets. We tie them together and stretch them across the branches. They will keep off any rain which comes straight down, and the heavy dews. We build up the sides with brushwood, and hollow out a place for our hips, and gather twigs and leaves for our pillows.

In the daytime we do Company drill, Swedish exercises and tactical training. We charge, take cover, advance slowly and at the double, practise rapid fire, and even have a musketry course. Fifteen rounds to the minute is the aim of the instructors. We fire at two, four, five and six hundred yards. The number of bull's-eyes decreases in inverse proportion to the distance.

There are some who cannot even hit the target at a hundred yards. They are the latest acquisition to the Battalion and have not had much training. They invariably close their eyes as the pressure on their fingers increases. While these men are receiving extra attention, the rest of us just loaf about. We lie on our backs looking up into the blue sky.

The bayonet-fighting instructors are the fiercest of all. 'In – out – on guard!' they shout. Then comes the command: 'A short jab at the right nipple – go!'

After that, we are shown how to parry and thrust, and how to crash the butt-end of our rifles into an opponent's face. It revolts us. We have done these things hundreds of times during practice, but we know that we shall never perform them even once in fact. But we have to jump to it like any rookies who have just joined up. Most of us have never used a bayonet in action. It is a much safer rule to shoot before you reach your opponent, or before he reaches you. The first thing we learnt in the Army was that the rifle was our best friend.

Then we are shown how to withdraw it if the bayonet gets stuck. But we shall never carry out these instructions either. If such a thing occurred, we should fire a shot or two, and so blow a hole which would make the withdrawal easier.

The instructor swears profusely and grows purple in the face.

He seems to lose all sense of proportion and go mad. But he must do these things, otherwise he would be of little value. Then he would be sent up to the trenches like the rest of us. So he uses up the daylight hours cursing and losing his temper, and his imagination seldom gets beyond a straw sack, either hanging or lying on the ground, and 'In – out – on guard!' When words fail him, he invariably ends with, 'You couldn't knock the skin off a good rice pudding!' When we hear these words we know that he has reached the end of his tether. It is the stock expression of physical training instructors.

When he has sufficiently wiped his forehead and finished glaring at us, he shows us how to disarm a man. The instructor always chooses the least proficient as his opponent. He rushes in, gives his arm a twist, and then grabs his rifle. The secret of securing the rifle seems to be to act unexpectedly and quickly. We have not yet come across a soldier who would let his enemy come sufficiently close to perform the act. The Germans do not like the bayonet. But neither do any of us for that matter, despite the Generals, far in the rear, and what they say in praise of it, and of the glory of a bayonet charge.

In tactical training, we advance at a given signal with our rifles at the trail. Short forward rushes are the rule. We rush a short distance, and drop when the whistle is blown. Then we lie perfectly still until it is sounded. In time, we reach our objective. We then repeat the operation, taking advantage of any small fold in the ground, or hiding behind any obstruction. We pant like dogs in the summer time, but when the whistle blows we must move quickly. If any man is slow in doing so, he is given twenty extra ups and downs. Old age, stiff muscles, mud or thorns are no excuse. So even though our hearts beat like sledge-hammers, we keep on going. It is quicker in the end.

When the Colonel comes along leisurely on horseback, the Company Officer redoubles his efforts. He is a small man and barks just like a terrier. He has spent twenty years of his life doing these things and acquiring an extensive vocabulary of sorts. Besides, he wears four ribbons on his left breast.

Then we advance slowly in extended order. A barrage is supposed to the falling in front of us, and we move almost at a snail's pace. This exercise is new to us. In action, we have been accustomed to go forward at a much quicker rate. Many of our men have been wounded by running into our own barrage, or by shells dropping behind them because they went forward too quickly. The new movement is calculated to avoid such losses in the future.

We see some sense in teaching us these things. Everything is timed exactly, and the infantry can work with the artillery. But it has taken the military mind an age to discover this elementary principle. Scores of thousands of men have been killed by our own artillery.

From nine in the morning until five in the afternoon we work at one thing or another. After that, some of us wander far into the wood in search of anything that will interest us.

When night comes, we lie in our bivouacs and talk. The theme is always the same. We discuss the war, and the reason why we are here. We wonder if Jerry passes the time in the same way. There is no reason to think that he behaves differently. He cannot like getting wet through any more than we do. It is as difficult for him to pull his large boots out of the mud as it is for us to pull out our rubber boots. The lice worry him as much as they worry us. His rations cannot come up through a barrage any more than ours can be brought up. A bursting shell, bomb or mortar must have the same effect upon him as upon us.

We know from experience that they are no different from ourselves. They have a sense of humour, and might easily have been for us instead of against us. A hundred years ago they were our allies. Now they are our enemies. We cannot think that the people have changed. It is the system that is at fault, or those who pull the strings behind the scenes. If the top six politicians from all the combatant countries were to spend twenty-four hours in the trenches, the war would end the following day.

The last time in the trenches, a Saxon shouted across to us, 'What time is tea coming up to-night, Tommy?' Perhaps he had worked in a hotel in London, or toured England with a German band. Many of them can speak our language and have visited our country. They did not meet with any hostility there. We are not ill-disposed towards them, and we believe that they feel just the same way towards us.

If there appeared to be an end of the matter it would be different. We could count off each day, and reckon up the fraction left. Then we could roughly estimate our chances of escape. But such a pastime is denied us, and we appear to be caught like rats in a trap. There is no escape possible for any of us. We decide that somebody is getting something out of it. It would not possibly last so long unless the politicians or Generals or munition-makers were gaining fame or riches.

Our personal gain has been nothing. At first, we were paid sixpence a day. Latterly, it has been increased to a shilling. That probably needed a special act of Parliament, and a good deal of wrangling. Out of our pay we buy all that is needed to keep ourselves clean. For it, we salute twice. We halt two paces from the pay table and salute. Then we move forward, and scoop the coins with the right hand into the left hand. Then we move back two paces and salute again. 'About-turn – quick march!' shouts the sergeant-major, and we make way for the next man. You must do this to get what is rightfully your own. One cannot be relied upon to say 'thank-you'. It is all double-march, and straight lines and discipline. Now, I can neither go forward nor backward of my own free will. I can only move when a thousand move. I can only move when I am told to move. I am no longer an entity, but a cog waiting to be set in motion.

We should be perfectly willing for the result to go by arbitration. Or, failing this, we could even suggest a much better way to end the war. If ten fire-eating Generals from each side could be nominated to fight it out, we are satisfied that it would end in ten minutes, and without a single casualty. A table, some glasses, and several quick-moving orderlies would be the only things necessary. Then we could all go home again.

CHAPTER THREE

The Sacrifice

We are in a shallow trench beside the La Bassée Canal. Westminster Bridge, a crossing over the canal, is only a few yards away. A mile ahead of us the Germans are attacking the village of Givenchy. The 55th (Lancastrian) Division is in the line there, and they are giving the Huns hell.

A battery of 18 pounders goes rushing past us. A few hundred yards over the bridge it swerves to the left and then stops. The horses are unhitched and in a few minutes the gunners are firing over open sights in answer to an SOS signal.

Wounded men pass by us. Some can manage to make their way to the dressing station without assistance. Others are leaning on a friend. At times one can see a blood-stained bandage. Jerries carry the stretcher cases. Sometimes they pull in to the side of the road and off-load a man. It is of no use to carry a dead person. A few minutes ago he was alive, and though his case was desperate it was not hopeless.

All day long we can hear the rat-tat-tat of machine-guns and the staccato crack from rifle fire. Towards evening the noise subsides. Then comes a sweet sickly scent from the forward positions. We all recognise it but do not talk about it. With darkness come the fireworks. Green, yellow, white and red flares; our own and theirs light up No-man's-land.

A German sergeant-major has given himself up, and said that there will be an attack in another part of the line. He has named the place, the day, and even the hour when the attack will take place. This makes the end of our stay on the canal bank.

We hand in our packs and overcoats, and are issued with extra ammunition. We are going to relieve the troops in the front line where the sergeant-major has said the attack will be made. Guides arrive to show us the way.

During our stay beside the canal none of us could have even dreamt that within a few days our platoon would have ceased to exist. It would be shot to pieces in No-man's-land, half-way between the British and the German front lines. We would be offered up as a sacrifice to the enemy gunners, and presented to them like John the Baptist's head on a platter.

On our left were mounds of broken bricks. They were all that was left of Festubert. There had been desperate fighting around this place earlier in the war, and the village had been destroyed. Now only soldiers lived in cellars there.

Between the front lines, which at this point were perhaps four hundred yards apart, there was a forward post in the middle of No-man's-land! Perhaps some theorist had drawn a sketch of the opposing front lines, and decided that it would serve a good purpose to station a platoon between them. Thus do the men in high places gamble with other people's lives. The post was about forty yards in length. The ground was low-lying and there were no trenches. If you dug a foot or fifteen inches, water came out and so the last state was worse than the first. For protection, men relied upon the ubiquitous sandbag, and built breastworks.

Here and there a tree-stump stuck up gauntly and appeared to lend some necessary support to the sandbags. But there was nothing that could withstand the 5.9's and minenwerfers. In only a few minutes they would make a shambles of this place.

The object of this forward position was that the occupants might hold up an enemy attack, and so give the men in the cellars, two hundred yards to the rear, an opportunity to get out when the barrage lifted, and come into action with their machine-guns. It was the brain-child of some General who would see the war through from some place far behind the line. Any private could have told him that before he attacked, the Hun would first reduce this post to rubble, and that when this had been done, his infantry would over-run it without opposition. However good the plan might be in theory, in practice it could not possibly work. Only after there had been forty human sacrifices would such a possibility dawn upon the originator of the scheme.

We moved silently across-country, and dropped into the listening post, to relieve the Liverpool Scottish. Those who were going out expressed no regret at having to leave the place. In an enemy attack it would be quickly over-run, they said, and the defenders would have little chance to escape. There was nothing one could do but hang on and sell one's life as dearly as possible. The chances of survival were ten thousand to one against in any betting man's book.

We settled down to await events. Two hundred yards away from an enemy one generally feels reasonably safe. It is too far away for a hand-grenade to come hurtling at you through the air.

The hours passed slowly. Down the slope Very lights shot up into the sky. By them one knew that the enemy was not abroad. This knowledge gave us confidence. Sometimes a voice could be heard.

The ration party came before dawn, and we shared out the bread, bacon, jam and cheese. A loaf to two men; a tin of jam among four; a lump of bacon and a slice of cheese to each man.

Besides, there were always the iron rations for an emergency. We had often fared much worse.

Some ate their rations for breakfast; others, more prudent, saved a little until later in the day. The first would feast, and then tighten their belts and starve philosophically. At least it would be so much less for Jerry to capture, they said. The others decided that a stomach wound would be less dangerous if one had not eaten to repletion. Besides, a square inch in the evening helps to shorten the night hours.

The sun rose and the day was quiet. A shell which seemed to have lost itself found its way across. Later, several screamed past, high overhead. The older soldiers said that the enemy gunners were registering, and that the next day the attack would be made.

We put up eight periscopes that morning. Each was smashed in turn. Enemy snipers were keeping a wide eye open upon the breastwork. A ping, and a shatter! Another one gone. There was none left for the afternoon, so we kept on our guard for any sound that might come across.

The enemy appeared to be rather lively. A command, a chuckle, or a guttural sentence could sometimes be heard. Jerry was becoming careless; or perhaps his nervousness was making him garrulous.

The troops have not yet been born who have not experienced a sense of fear before an attack upon the enemy. If you knew the worst, you might become reconciled to the inevitable. But a foot to the right or left, or two yards in advance or behind the others might make all the difference. You might get a comfortable flesh wound, or you might lose half your face. One has plenty to think about.

It is always a bad sign when things are quiet. So long as a trench-mortar shell or a whizz-bang comes occasionally, or a rifle or a machine-gun opens up on you, you know that you are safe. you know that the enemy is only firing to keep up his spirits, like a small boy who whistles as he walks along a dark lane.

That night, the ration party came again with their sand-bags. At the Front, sand-bags served many purposes. Filled with earth, they protected the outer man; filled with bread, they fortified the inner man. Bread, boiled bacon, cheese, tins of beans, and issue of cigarettes were hastily dumped. Hurriedly the carriers dropped their load and departed. One never lingers at a listening post. A cellar, covered by six feet of bricks, is a safer place then an open trench. It was too dark to share out the rations, so we dumped them on the parados or rear of the breastwork. Then we waited; waited for daylight.

At half-past four in the morning, the enemy batteries started firing. The sky seemed full of shells. The high-velocity shells caused you to duck, though they passed high overhead. They were directed elsewhere; they hurried on to the Divisional battery positions. In a moment or two it was like hell let loose. Away to the front you saw a flash, and almost instantaneously you heard a scream as the shell cleaved the air and then came to earth behind you. The roar of the burst told you that the casualty list was growing.

In the meantime, we sat undisturbed in our breastwork. There was nothing to do but to stay where you were. The battle had begun.

Howitzer fired upon howitzer; whiz-bang fired upon eighteen-pounder. You sat in the darkness, knowing that in a few hours your turn would come. Those who had cigarettes lit them. The soldier said that a smoke steadied the nerves. Perhaps the greatest value of a cigarette was that it gave you something to do. You had to do something to light it; you had to do something to smoke it. There are few things that are as harmful at times as inactivity.

For two hours the sky seemed full of shells, but they all appeared to go in only one direction. One guessed that our own artillery was conserving the ammunition in order to break up the enemy's attack when it should come.

At 6.30 a.m. the range shortened, and the barrage came down upon the listening-post and the front line. In five minutes there was scarcely one sand-bag resting upon another. Heavies, whiz-bangs, minenwerfers, rifle grenades and machine-gun bullets came from everywhere. It was full daylight, and you saw the destruction going on all about you. Jerry was not leaving anything to chance. His infantry would have an easy and safe passage through our breastwork. There would be nobody there to stop him.

The scorching fumes choked you. The chunks of shrapnel whizzed past you with a noise like that of a screeching tram-car as it gathers speed. The heavies convulsed the earth, and a pile of débris rose and fell on you. The murderous field-gun, perhaps the most hated of all enemy weapons, hissed and murdered. The machine-gunners were traversing, or sweeping, the ground, so that you could not move. They pinned you to earth.

Trench-mortar shells could be seen as they twisted through the air towards you at a height of only a hundred feet. As they fell, they joined in with everything else that was falling, and were lost in the holocaust.

Every square foot of ground was swept with shot. One would think that a mouse running for cover would find none anywhere. We crouched and wished that we could halve our size. At such times one gets very close to earth.

Away to the right and to the left, men fall and are seen no more. A fraction of a second is sufficient. A potential hero can offer no more resistance than the least soldierly of the platoon. It is luck, sheer luck, that you find yourself uninjured from moment to moment.

The listening-post quickly becomes a bloody shambles. Forty-four men have been greatly divided. You cannot count who are left, but momentarily you catch a glimpse of a face, and you mentally register that he is still unhit. All the while the bombardment continues. You think that men were never intended to live in this way, or even to die so violently. The noise is so terrific that your head nearly bursts. A mouthful of scorching sulphur or lyddite causes you to choke.

Three yards away from where I lie behind the stump of a tree, Private Jack Squance can stand it no longer. He jumps up and you wonder what he is going to do. He, himself, seems quite undecided; he must do something – anything. But he does not have to make up his mind. A screaming whizz-bang travelling almost parallel to the ground decides the matter. The trunk falls, headless. One more casualty. His parents will never know what happened to him.

The hangers-on are becoming fewer; only twenty-one are left. Instinctively they draw closer together.

The Lewis gun team hangs together. Sergeant Newman, in charge of it, has become a casualty. He did not suffer. A shell, quite large, pinned him through the chest, where he sat and waited. It did not explode. It was only a dud, but it claimed him. He lies only a few yards away. The other gunners have moved down a little; they do not look backwards. It is better not to do so. His brother, Lance-corporal 'Navvy' Newman, goes and runs up and down until he is also killed. They were both regular soldiers, and in the Battalion at the beginning of the war.

The platoon officer, 2nd Lieutenant Hudson, joins me. He crawls on all fours, keeping as close to the ground as possible. He is not very much more than twenty years old. We have been friends; he is a very nice fellow. We talk, and decide to send up the first SOS signal. It soars up into the sky, then falls. The artillery observers will have seen it.

The reply should come soon. One would be able to detect the shells going over to the enemy. They do not come. We fire a second rocket; it is unanswered. A third goes up – it is the last we have. There is no answer to it. Something must have happened. It is the first time the Divisional artillery has failed the front-line infantry. Again and again they have replied to the distress signal; at Ypres, Loos, the Somme – they returned two shells for one.

The Lewis gun team has not moved far enough down. They were not to know such a thing. One spot is the same as another, if your luck is in. A 5.9 falls close to them. It is practically a direct hit. They are wiped out completely. Two have not been hit, but the concussion was sufficient. They just sleep. You cannot see any mark upon them. It is brutal, terrible, wholesale slaughter.

The two boxes of reserve ammunition have been blown up. The gun may still be of service. Private Disley and another man volunteer to go back to Company Headquarters for further supplies of ammunition. They jump up, and disappear into a hail of shells. You would think that no living thing could get far. The shells seem to search them out. We can see them at times when the smoke clears a little. They vanish into the tornado with one chance in a thousand of arriving at their destination. Perhaps they think that there is as much safety in moving as in cowering behind sand-bags.

In twenty minutes they are back again. They have passed twice through the barrage; it is a miracle. They bring back an ammunition box given to them by the Company Captain and the sergeant-major.

We force open the box. It is not heavy enough for ammunition. Inside, there are only Very lights. There is no hope of holding up the enemy when he comes over. Our Lewis gun has been knocked out; the stock and barrel are yards apart. It would be useless, even if the ammunition had reached us.

The platoon officer suggests that we should retire and join the remainder of the Company in the cellars. We take a last look towards the enemy lines as the shelling seems to be dying down, or the range has increased. Fewer shells are now falling upon us.

The attack has begun. It is 8.20 by the watch. Every twenty yards or less, an enemy machine-gun is in action. They have come out of their trench, and opened fire upon the listening-post. We have heard of this method of attack; infiltration, they call it.

They are only a hundred yards away. Then comes the infantry advance. One sees the field-grey uniforms come slowly over. They walk as though the rest of the day belongs to them. The machine-guns cover their advance. All around us the bullets go zip-zip-zip. The air is full of the sound. How we hate the machine-gunners!

Our officer shouts a final 'Run for it!' He leads the way. There are only eight of us left; seven besides himself. I am the youngest of them. We scramble over mounds of earth, and take little notice of our comrades. Most of them are beyond help; we still live.

We disappear down a shell-hole, and appear again on the other side. The machine-gun bullets search us out. We keep together, but do not bunch up. It is safer to do this, though there seems to be little safety anywhere. You hear the zips as the bullets pass you; they are at all levels. We zig-zag, which makes the shooting more difficult.

There may be many guns firing upon us, and each sends out hundreds of bullets a minute. There seems little chance of our getting out of it alive.

Our speed is slackened as we come to a marsh. We have lost direction, and are knee deep in water and mud. It becomes deeper as we go forward, but we cannot go back, and it might be worse if we turn to the right or left.

One of us is hit in the knee. Another crumples up with a smashed shoulder. We cannot stay to bandage them up; we can only support them and go forward. The water becomes discoloured as we take our two wounded comrades through the swamp.

We come out on the other side. We are exhausted and cannot

go much further. Ahead of us is a pile of old planks. We make for it, and rest on the far side of it, for it gives reasonable cover. Besides, the wounded cannot walk any more and we cannot carry them. We must be well within our own lines. The machine-gun fire becomes less. A stray shot comes our way.

Away on the right, and then on the left, we hear the Lewis guns come into action. They fire at the rate of six hundred bullets a minute. One can tell the difference between these and the enemy guns. Ours fire more rapidly; theirs have more precision. Both are equally deadly.

The firing goes on for nearly an hour. It is long since our gunners have had such targets and such a favourable field of fire. There are thousands of Boches in the attack; they are in mass-formation, and our gunners cannot miss them!

By ten o'clock the firing dies down. After that, one hears only a sniper's bullet. The action is over. The enemy has again failed to break through. The Battle of Bethune has ended disastrously for the Germans. Their losses have been enormous. The field is strewn with grey corpses. In places, they are piled high upon one another. Here they have been enfiladed. Sometimes the heaps surge; the badly-wounded move, and try to rid themselves of the weight upon them.

One hears many sounds. They all mean cries for help. The stretcher-bearers from both sides go out into No-man's-land. No one fires upon them. It will be many hours before the field is cleared; and many who might be rescued will not be alive the next day. There is so much work to do. The bad cases are attended to first, but there are so many of them. The stretcher-bearers take the nearest ones. The cries for help continue all day and into the night. Only when all the wounded have been attended to will the dead be collected and carried back.

The Divisional artillery have had very many casualties. It was chiefly yellow-cross gas which the enemy fired. That was why our SOS signals were unanswered. In time everything becomes clear.

We have been relieved and move back to Gorre. On the way we are astounded to see our platoon officer. He is lying on the edge of a deep shell-hole. The head is nearly severed from the body. It dips down into the shell-hole. One hand is held to the wrist by a single tendon. The soil is wet beneath his head and wrist.

We find a stretcher and put him on it. The ground has been torn up and it is heavy work even with four men. But we would willingly have carried him twenty miles.

CHAPTER FOUR

Battery and Assault

Along this part of the Front it looks as if a tornado has struck a hundred times. All around us there are ruins. We have come to the south of the La Bassée Canal and relieved the Sherwood Foresters. Beside us is a signboard marked 'Cuinchy', but nothing is now left of the village. There are only trenches, deep shell-holes, large craters, and miles of barbed wire.

The twentieth century savages have left their trade-mark. Here, the Prussians, the Wurtembergers, Bavarians and Saxons have goose-stepped in their arrogance and destroyed in their anger.

Many thousands of our men have fallen along this lengthy sector. The place is really a vast cemetery. The whole region smells like an abattoir. No one would choose to spend a single day here. It is a hell-hole. No one who has been in the line in this place, and survived, has left it as completely whole as when he came in.

We have three main lines of defence. They are the front line, the support line and the reserve line. In the first two lines there are dug-outs. Some of them face the wrong way. These are in German trenches which have been stormed and held. The reserve line is a tunnel and is well underground, with steps at intervals leading up to the surface. The tunnel is always full of weary men.

The place is a labyrinth of smaller connecting trenches. Each has a name, clearly marked, but without a map or a guide we should lose ourselves. Even our guides sometimes manage to lose both themselves and us. Then comes the command 'About turn!', and we retrace our steps until we come to some recognisable spot, and then begin all over again.

Any kind of name seems to have been given to these trenches. We read Glasgow Road, Hertford Street, Berkshire Road, Marylebone Road, Praed Street, Pudding Lane, Lover's Lane, Coldstream Lane, Clive Road, Kingsway, Back Street, Cabbage Patch, Old Kent Road and a host of other names.

The terrorists have come to life again. On all sides the gongs are sounding. It is late afternoon, and a gentle breeze is blowing from the east. The day has been relatively quiet, but we all feel that this is much too good to last. Around six o'clock someone shouts 'Gas!' Then we hear the gongs again come into service. This is normal practice, and the recognised way of warning everybody in the area.

For a mile or more along our line we are on the alert. Blankets are slung over the dug-out openings, and cover them completely. Water is thrown on the blankets until they drip. All those who are on sentry-duty are at their posts, and will quickly tell us if an attack is about to be launched. There have been signs of restiveness for several days, and we wonder if the Huns are coming over.

A dozen of us are sitting on a fire-step in the support line. Our rifles are resting on the parapet, with bayonets fixed. Our satchels are open, and in a moment we can extract our gas masks. But we decide to await events. If the gas is chlorine we shall whip out the masks and wear them.

The German front line is at least three hundred yards away from us, and has probably been vacated while the gas is being sent over. We decide to have a look at No-man's-land. It may be a foolish thing to do, but it is not often that we can have a grandstand view of anything happening on the battlefield.

Little shells are bursting all around us, but none come our way. The nearest lands twenty-five yards from where we are. We hear a 'plop' and duck our heads below the parapet. Then we look out again, but nothing is moving. It is almost like a game of hide-and seek, and, childlike, we enjoy the little diversion.

There is no smell of chlorine. We recognise the gas as tear gas, and still do not put on our masks. As the tears stream down our cheeks, it is as though we weep but do not cry. There is a pleasant scent all about us, but it will not hang around for many hours as a heavier gas would do. Hundreds of men along the sector are experiencing the same discomfort, but none are choking. We know that this gas is not a lethal one, and that in an hour or two its effects will wear off. We know, too, that the enemy will pay heavily for this attack on us. No assault of any kind ever goes unrequited. The old Biblical maxim of an eye for an eye and a tooth for a tooth operates all the time with us. As soon as conditions are favourable, our own gas squads will move in and drench the German lines. Fatigue parties will bring up the drums of gas by the hundred to our front line. Then the experts will take over. We hope that no shells will fall upon us before the gas can be discharged. This is a risk that has to be taken. If shrapnel were to pierce the drums, we should be in big trouble, and hoist on our own petard.

We appear to be well on the way to becoming dehumanised. All our early training and education was aimed at creating and building up, but now we seek only to destroy. Pity seems to be going out of our nature. The more we can injure the other man, the more satisfied we become. Our aim is always to strike two blows to his one.

When we are in the line and have nothing better to do, we sometimes discuss this matter. Half a dozen of us get together, and we hold forth in turn. 'Whichever way you look at it', I say, 'soldiering has always been a brutal affair. Coarse work always makes coarse people, and if we stay in this game much longer, it will mark us for life.'

Moore agrees with me. Normally this Londoner is a rather shy and retiring man who thinks a lot but does not often express an opinion. On this subject he freely airs his thoughts. 'Take that Sergeant, for instance', he says, 'his whole life is centred around the bayonet and how best to drive it into some unfortunate fellow's vitals. He says that three inches of cold steel are generally enough, but that six inches of it are better still. His whole attitude is one of aggressiveness, and he tries to instil his fighting spirit into us. Up to a point, he succeeds. He has become a butcher, and seeks to make butchers of us all. Whether we like it or not, we are on the way downhill. The slide has begun.'

'It's the only way to deal with these bloody Huns,' says Williams. 'They're a lot of bastards. Always on the rampage and looking for trouble like their namesakes who were the Asiatic invaders of Europe in the fourth century, in the time of Attila the Hun. Why the hell did they have to plough their way through Belgium in '14 and bring us all into this mess? They've always been bad neighbours, and wanting other people's possessions. They've steam-rollered their way through up to now. It is high time somebody stood up to these bullies. Force is the only thing they can understand. That's why we are here.'

'Edmund Burke wrote that you cannot indict a whole nation', I say.

Replies the inexorable Williams, 'He was referring to the Yanks, and not to these lice. In any case, he didn't say that you cannot indict ninety per cent of a nation. And that is exactly what I say; they're fit for one thing, and one thing only, and that is extermination.'

Jackson is less forceful than Williams, but more gentle and

scholarly. 'What I don't understand', he says, 'is how a great people can have these periodical outbursts of madness. Why is it that a whole nation can support this kind of venture? Has all reason deserted them? Don't they realize that some day and somewhere they will be stopped? What happened to the far-flung Roman Empire? And the conquests of Ghengis Khan and Alexander? Must a nation which has produced so many great men seek its own destruction in this way? Does history cease to have a meaning?'

Thompson sums it up in his own inimitable way. 'As I see it', he says, 'they are a hard and tough people, but lack a sense of humour. They have too great a respect for authority and a uniform, and have become an entirely subservient people. They are really a pack of wolves, but behave like sheep when some high-up comes on the scene. Just look at how they treat their womenfolk! Even the meanest among them lords it over his wife, as if he owns her. An Emperor can do no wrong. Neither can a military leader. The iron has entered into their souls, but still they cringe. And they always will. They have produced brilliant men, but been a menace for far too long.'

Our lives are divided into cycles of sixteen days. We spend four of them in each of the three lines, and then go back to one of the villages like Annequin or Cambrin for the other four. In Cambrin our billet is a cellar. The house has been destroyed, but a few feet of the front wall remains. We eat all our meals here, and a few planks resting on bricks form our dining-room table. On three sides there is nothing but rubble, and overhead only the sky.

Our days are free, and we spend a part of each one asleep in the cellar. It is dark down there, but candles are plentiful and cheap. There is a canteen in the village and we can buy cigarettes, plug tobacco, matches, stationery, and certain foodstuffs there.

The canteen is heavily boarded up and sand-bagged. A screen of hessian has been placed around it as a precaution, for the troops come and go there all day long, and it is under observation from the enemy lines. We play cards, or write letters home, or do a little reading to pass the time. No serious reading is possible as there are too many interruptions.

When night comes, our work begins. All supplies for the trenches have to be carried forward, and we stagger along with rolls of barbed wire, or bundles or iron pickets five feet long, or boxes of ammunition or hand-grenades or rations.

A German airman has been brought down. On two consecutive days he has chanced his arm and got away with it. He has come streaking right along our front line, and cannot have been more than a hundred feet above our heads. With the engine screaming and his machine-gun pouring bullets down upon us, he has come out of the north like a flash of lightning. It is a terror tactic, and brilliantly carried out. We admire the pilot's skill and daring. He is clearly a master of his craft.

He follows our line until he is over Vermelles, and then the plane rises high into the sky and swings eastward. Our anti-air-craft guns open up and we see little puffs of black smoke, but the gunners are firing more in hope than in expectation. The airman twists and turns and dives and climbs until he is out of range. He is as elusive as a snipe, and as difficult to bring down.

On the third day fortune does not favour the brave. We hear the plane coming from afar. Every man in the line has fifteen rounds in the magazine of his rifle, and the Vickers and Lewis guns are also ready and waiting.

For several days we have been expecting a big German attack in this sector, and the Machine-Gun Company has been brought in to help us in repelling it. No attack has developed, but the reliable Vickers now come into their own. The riflemen open rapid fire as the shrieking plane comes in like a bat out of hell. All the machine-guns bark defiance, and tracer bullets guide the fire of the men behind them. No airman has ever run into bigger trouble. A wall of bullets bars his way. They come in from all angles. We see the will-o'-the-wisp tracers shining in the sun like silver darts. The plane is enveloped in them.

The din is terrific. A thousand or two thousand rifles are firing simultaneously, and fifty machine-guns are in action. Every one of us is determined that the airman shall not pass this way again. Escape is impossible. No amount of courage will avail against this concentrated fire.

A long trail of smoke can be seen as the plane streaks past us. A cheer goes up all along our line. The firing goes on as the pilot loses height, and then swerves to the left. We see the plane crashing behind the German lines over towards La Bassée. It is on fire, and is like a shooting star. It explodes on hitting the ground, and a sheet of flame rises from it. A pillar of black smoke marks the funeral pyre.

The airman has had his last flight. We have admired his prowess and daring, and in a sense we are sorry to see his demise. But it was inevitable. If he had come in the opposite direction, and an hour earlier or later, his luck might have held. He might then have caught us off our guard, and run into only half of the hail of lead which was poured into him and his machine. Perhaps it was contempt for the shooting of the men on the ground which led to this repeat performance of the act, and to his own undoing.

The German troops in the lines opposite to us have had the same view of the exciting spectacle as we have had, and three times in three days they have experienced a thrill at our discomfiture. They must feel sore at heart that this drama has ended in an anti-climax, as the curtain comes down on the last act and their hero is shot down.

We think that this attack from above has solved one of our problems. Jerry will now know with what strength we are holding the line, and use his massed infantry in some other part. To come over at us here would be an act of madness. We speculate on whether or not it may have been his method of finding out how our line is held, and so assess the possibility of success in an infantry assault upon it, by sending the airman to draw our fire. If so, the loss of one man and one plane for the knowledge gained will have solved one of his problems too. If this really was the intention, it was a wily and clever move, and cheap at the price paid. He will never make a better bargain.

Two of our men are dead. They were caught in a burst from the airman's machine-gun as the plane swept over their heads. We place them aside in the trench, and cover each of them with a blanket. Stretcher-bearers will come up when it is dark, and they will be carried back to behind the lines for burial.

We know that Jerry will not let the shooting down of the airman go unpunished. Some form of retribution will surely follow. We should do the same ourselves. And knowing from the volume of our firing that our three lines are packed with troops, he will make the penalty a very severe one if he can possibly do so. There is also the matter of maintaining the morale of his own infantry. The men in the line always have their tails well up when they know that those opposite them are taking a pasting.

In the middle of the afternoon comes the deluge, but arrangements have been made to counter such a happening. Our men have nearly all gone underground. The dug-outs are crammed with them. A single look-out man stands on the fire-step in every third bay and will immediately give the alarm if he sees the enemy swarm out of their trenches. As the barrage is lifted, the dug-outs will disgorge their occupants, and No-man's-land will be littered with German dead.

When the first shell falls, the rush for safety begins. As usual, the gunners are right on their target and our line is blasted unmercifully. On our right someone sends up an SOS flare. It rises quickly and burns brightly. Within a minute our field artillery comes into action. From in front of us come the 5.9's and the whizz-bangs. From behind us come the 4.5's and the screeching 18-pounders. It is an evenly-matched duel.

In twenty minutes the firing dies down and then ceases. But the dirty brown-black fumes from bursting shells hang over us like a thick London fog in mid-winter. Only when the wind rises and disperses them can we breathe freely again. Our trenches are a shambles. They have been blown in in a hundred places. It will take large fatigue parties many days to repair the damage and put up new belts of wire entanglements in front of them.

Jerry is in no better case. His lines are hidden from us by the static smoke, but we know that he has had the same pounding as ourselves. Neither side has gained anything. Not even a foot of ground has been lost or won. Another fifty or hundred thousand pounds have gone down the drain. The hospitals receive the wounded, and the cemeteries the dead.

We count our dead and gather the wounded. Over the way, the Jerries are doing it too. Neither we nor they think of molesting one another. Night comes down gradually on the battlefield. At intervals green and yellow flares shoot up from the enemy lines. Jerry is a suspicious man and is not taking any chances.

D Company is to carry out a raid. We shall be immediately on their right. A and C Companies are in support. It is said that the object of the raid is to capture a prisoner for identification. We do not believe that this can really be the reason as only a few nights ago we found a couple of stiffs in No-man's-land. We were out on patrol and came upon them. They were dead, and lying in a shell-hole near our wire. This might be why their comrades had not found them and taken them away. We searched them and took their identity discs and papers. They were all handed in so the big shots who are handling this show already know which regiment is opposite to us. But even if other troops have come in in the meantime, there would be less hazardous and costly ways of bringing in a prisoner.

Our Company heads for the front line. D Company is already there. We move out of our cellars and are almost immediately in Bomb Alley. Then comes Hertford Street, and we know that we are nearing our destination. From here on, strict silence is maintained. We pass into Clive Road, and space ourselves out at the end of the trench. The German front line is only thirty yards away from us at this point. We are in a sap projecting outwards towards it.

At half-past nine our artillery opens fire. In half-an-hour it will be dark, and the raiders will then retire to their own line. It is hoped that the darkness will enable them to get back safely. We believe that this is wishful thinking.

The shells go crashing down in three lines. It is a box barrage. The first line is ahead of our infantry. The other two are along the flanks. The Germans within the box are sealed off, and can only escape by running through the barrage. The alternative is to stand and fight it out as the men of D Company go forward into the cauldron with grenades, fixed bayonets, and with great resolution.

We cannot see anything of what is happening over there, although it is only a couple of hundred yards away from us. The bursting shells and deepening twilight enfold everything. But we can tell that some intense tragedy is being played albeit on a limited scale.

The barrage increases in volume until it becomes drum-fire. Our troops go forward and bomb the dug-outs. We give covering fire, and every one of us lets off fifteen rounds a minute. It is rapid fire, and continuous. There are many open boxes of ammunition beside us. If any of the enemy should break out in our direction we should get them all. Our fire is directed beyond the forward line of the box to make the defenders keep their heads down. Shrapnel scatters in all directions there, and if any Huns come out of the inferno alive, there will be many head wounds. Rarely, if ever, have our gunners laid on a more telling barrage.

Red flares go up all along the enemy line where our troops are attacking. They are the call for immediate help. The ever-watchful German gunners answer the call and lay down a curtain of bursting shells which the men of D Company must pass through when the fighting ceases.

By ten o'clock there is complete darkness and the raid is over. We have no means of knowing what has happened, and cannot form an opinion as to whether the raid has been worthwhile or not. Even those who have been in the raiding party are not able to give an accurate overall picture. In the race against time none of them goes down into the dug-outs to count the dead. They throw their hand-grenades into them, but do not know if they are occupied or deserted. The men in the front line only know about things that are happening in their immediate vicinity.

Within twenty-four hours Jerry hits back at us. There is a terrific explosion fifty yards along our trench, and someone calls for stretcher-bearers. We rush along to give assistance, and find one man dead and two others badly wounded. One of them cannot be moved. He has been hit in the stomach and also lower down. There is a large gaping wound in the right groin. Nothing can be done for him. The other wounded man has lost his left foot. We pour iodine into the wound. Then he is quickly bandaged and carried away to the dressing-station. We dig out three men who are buried. They are not injured, but are very badly shocked. They tremble all over, and cannot utter a word.

A minenwerfer falling right on the parapet has made this part of the trench a shambles. Before we can send the three shell-shocked men back for attention, another mortar bomb comes over. But it bursts well beyond us and does no harm to anybody.

It will be many weeks before the three men rejoin us. They are in a bad way. These nerve cases are the very devil. We have had them before. When any man has had such an experience he becomes transformed, and is never more than half a soldier afterwards. He ducks and falls to the ground if a shell bursts even a hundred yards away. If you fire a rifle near him, the sharp crack nearly makes him jump out of his skin. It is a reflex action, and he can no more control it than fly to the moon.

We hate these trench-mortars almost as much as the 5.9's. They are just as devastating. For twenty minutes we are kept on the run. At times two or three mortars are in the air at the same time. We see them coming from the moment they leave the machines in the German line, and we scuttle to left and right seeking to put a traverse between ourselves and the mortars.

Three men misjudge the direction and speed of a falling mortar. It requires split-second timing. We call to them loudly to turn back, but it is too late. The bomb comes down into a fire-bay just as they round a traverse and enter the bay. With a mighty roar the mortar explodes. There is no need for either stretcher-bearers or a burial party. Everything disintegrates.

There is a large hole blasted out of the bottom of the fire-bay. It is three feet deep and several feet across. Two corpses are lying in it. They have been there for a year or more. Their uniform is a greyish-blue. They are French troops who were killed and buried here. Now they have been disinterred and will have to be buried again. We cannot do it while the minenwerfers are coming over. It will not do them any harm to wait a few hours for a working party to arrive and shovel the earth back into the hole. If another bomb should come over in the meantime, it is not likely to fall in the same spot again. But even if this should happen it would make no difference as the dead have been dead a very long time.

Away on our right somebody is taking a terrific pounding. We cannot tell what it is all about as it is happening a mile or two from where we are. It is late at night, and our front line bends around over there. The night is peaceful for us, but we can see the darkness pierced by a hundred fires in an unbroken line. The cannonade works up to a crescendo. A Company or even a Battalion might be engaged. The fires mark the position of massed batteries of field-guns and howitzers, and vary in height and intensity. They look like a cross-section of some mountain range, or a chart of a place that experiences extreme temperatures. As one fire dies down, it is immediately followed by another. And above the line of fire there is a display of flares. They are orange, green and red. Our trench is crowded, and we watch the bombardment like men over whom some spell has been cast. We have not been told anything about our own men making an attack on the enemy. Neither do we know if the cannonade is on our Divisional front. It might be many months before we shall again see anything as spectacular as this night's display.

The gunners work feverishly for more than half-an-hour. This is drumfire. No sooner has one shell been fired than another is slammed into the breech of every gun and discharged. There is an unbroken rumble as of thunder in a tropical storm, from the barking guns and exploding shells. The PBI (Poor Bloody Infantry) – whoever they may be – will be cowering in their trenches and thinking that the end of the world has come. And for many, it will mean that this is the last time in the line.

How well do we know what they are experiencing! How well do we know what they are thinking! We have been in the same predicament ourselves, and wondered if we could possibly survive the ordeal by blast and tearing shrapnel.

There will be half-men and quarter-men and no men at all left where little groups now huddle together with a few planks or a sheet of elephant iron over them in a trench. When the firing dies down, the stretcher-bearers will be in great demand. They will gather up those who still cling to life, however tenuously. The field dressing-stations will be crowded, and the medical men and orderlies will go all out to save the wounded, and then send them down to the casualty clearing stations. Many of them will be back in the line again in a few months' time. Only death or total disablement will put an end to their misery.

The dead will be collected in due course. A deep trench will be dug behind the lines, and all the human debris of this part of the battlefield will be deposited in it.

CHAPTER FIVE

Holding the Line

We have lately come into what is reported to be a comfortable part of the line. It is the Cambrin right sub-sector. In the early part of the war it was the scene of much bitter fighting, but the position has been stalemate for quite a long time.

Both sides are well entrenched, and an attack here would be a costly affair. There is line after line of trenches, with communications leading from all angles. The place is a maze of trenches, with listening-posts and strong points everywhere. The trenches are, on the whole, easily six or seven feet deep. They are wide and well-formed. Here and there, they have fallen in or been blown in. Sometimes these points have been re-made; sometimes it has not been thought necessary to join them up again.

The enemy is about three hundred yards away. But in places he is much nearer. Opposite us he has a listening-post on the lip of a crater. We have one too. We believe that he only occupies his post at night. We occupy ours both by day and night. The crater is about the length of a cricket pitch from lip to lip. We hear his machine-gun firing every night from this forward post. It fires in short bursts and the bullets go zipping overhead. If we are on the fire-step, we keep our heads down. It would be suicidal to do otherwise. We listen for any raiding party who might come over. To find out if he was there in the daytime, the fearless 2nd Lieutenant Hampson and I crawled down the crater one afternoon. It took us almost an hour to make the journey there, and back. There was no one in the trench.

All the troops coming into this sector move along Lewis Alley. It is a long communication trench, and reaches as far as the tunnel. At the entrance to the tunnel there is a water point. The supply of water is tainted. It contains chloride of lime, but this is better than shell-hole water. It is safer. So we fill our water bottles from the tank there.

You can easily stand upright in the tunnel. Only in a few places do you have to stoop. There is always a light where you have to bend. Several men could pass each other in it. It is far below the ground, and you are entirely safe from shell-fire or from bombs dropped from aeroplanes. So we like being there.

The tunnel is not altogether pleasant. Its walls are of earth and it is constantly dripping water. The walls are covered with fungus growths, and it is not well ventilated. It is damp and clammy. But we do not mind that. Duck-boards line the tunnel from side to side, and we soon become accustomed to sleeping on them. Our hips ache, but that is a small price to pay for safety. We would gladly stay here for the duration.

Our only enemy here is the rats. Their number is legion. They are enormous things. The struggle for existence is not severe near the front line. Nearly every day we kill them, but their number does not seem to become smaller. They can learn from experience, and become scarce for a day or two after we organise a hunt. Then they return. We keep the lids on our mess tins always in the tunnel.

Here, we usually sleep in the daytime. We just lie down where we find ourselves. Troops passing by try to step over us. It is not often that we are trodden on, but occasionally somebody yells out,

'Take those bloody big clod-hoppers off my hand! You clumsy bugger, take them off!' I pull my waterproof sheet up over my face, and rest my head in an inverted steel helmet. My hands I always put into my trousers pockets. In this way, the skin is not exposed to the rats. When things are quiet, they run about in search of food. You feel them run over you, but you just kick out and scare them away. They come back again. In time, you become accustomed to them, do not mind them very much.

At night we leave the tunnel and do fatigue work. This usually consists of going back to the terminus of the light railway, at the point where the communication trench begins.

At eight o'clock the trolley comes back. We have to be there to meet it and help to unload it. There are all kinds of things on it; supplies of barbed wire, boxes of ammunition, boxes of hand-grenades, iron stakes – four and six feet long – the post, rations, canteen supplies, lime, and everything else that is necessary to maintain life for another day. About eight miles of the front are served by this railway.

We take up our loads and a guide shows us where to go. We disappear into the tunnel and stumble along. The barbed wire is in heavy rolls. We push a stick through the hole in the middle. Two men can carry two rolls in this way. It is the only way to manage such an unwieldy load. The barbs are an inch in length and often pierce one's hands and arms when a roll slides along the stick. Then there is much blaspheming.

The main tunnel has smaller tunnels leading from it. Each has its own name, otherwise we should easily get lost. Sometimes the guide stops, and wonders whether to go straight on or turn to the right. We do not interfere as it is his job to find the way. We only swear when we find that he has lost himself and us. The wire is heavy, and the fatigue ends when we reach our destination. You have to get a chit from the Commander of the Company when you hand over the goods.

Enemy trench-mortars have been destroying the wire, and we have to put up some new entanglements. It is a risky job at any time. The section to be wired is only fifty yards from Jerry's machine-guns. He has made a strong point near some brick stacks, and every night we hear his machine-gun fire coming from there.

We do not like this part of the front; one always feels that something is about to happen. The atmosphere seems super-charged, just as on a hot day before a storm. The nerves become frayed.

At ten o'clock we creep out over the top. There are about thirty of us. Some are carrying wire, while others have iron standards. The standards have a loop at the top for a stick to pass through. You twist the stick, and force in the standard. It would not be possible to knock them in; the noise would be too great, and the enemy would hear the work in progress. Jerry is quick on the uptake and never leaves anything to chance. He always reacts violently to any noise at night.

When we have gone twenty yards out of our trench, we stop. It is far enough. Besides, we want to finish the job. There are forty rolls of wire to be put up before dawn. Some of us take the standards and others unroll the wire. Two men to a roll is the easiest way to do it. A few of us hook the wire to the uprights. One has to be careful, as the barbs are both long and sharp.

We work for half-an-hour or more, until someone drops an iron stake. The clatter sounds terrific in the still night. Immediately we fall to earth and do not move. This is instinctive reaction to danger.

The enemy have heard the noise; perhaps they suspect a wiring party is out. They fire many flares in our direction, but do not see any signs of life. We lie as still as dormice. A machine-gun rakes the parapet of our trench, but the bullets go over us.

Presently the firing stops, and all becomes quiet again. We

carry on with our work, but not for long. In a few minutes the sky is lit up with flares. I am not quick enough; one bursts into flame before I fall. There is only one thing to do. One must not move. So I remain standing, and see the flame become brighter as the flare rises. Then it descends, coming always in my direction.

You can die many times in twenty seconds. Momentarily, I expect to hear the bullets. They do not come. The flare falls ten yards in front of me. As it strikes the earth, it fizzles out. Then I fall to the ground, almost scared out of my senses. I lie doggo, scarcely breathing.

A few yards have made all the difference. Had it fallen behind me, it would have been a different matter. Its own brilliance hid me from view. But I know that several German sentries are keeping a sharp look-out for any signs of movement in No-man's-land.

All is deadly quiet. After what seems an age, I whisper the names of those who have come out with me to put up the wire. I call one and then another, but get no reply. Then it becomes clear that they have gone back to the trench. I did not hear them go.

It is not easy to find the way back in the darkness, but I decide to make the attempt as the enemy might send out a patrol. I crawl on all fours, at first very slowly. Then I make my way as quietly and quickly as possible, still keeping close to the ground. Finally, when I judge that our trench can only be a few yards away, I run for it. I fall headlong into the trench, pick myself up again, and run farther.

The night is inky-black, and I stumble over a roll of wire which has been thrown away by our men when they retired. Again I jump up, thinking the enemy is upon me, and run anywhere until I see a light. It is in the support line, two hundred yards behind our trench. I stay there until dawn, then find my way back again to our post in the front line.

Twice a day we are shelled. At six in the morning, and again at seven in the evening, they come over. You could set your watch by them. Sometimes they send over some gas. It is chiefly tear-gas. You weep without realizing what you are doing. It is not bad enough to put on your mask. The gas shells are small and just make a half-noisy and half-quiet pop. The Front smells sweet and sickly. It is like very cheap scent. It is more irritable than dangerous. We call it pineapple gas.

Very rarely the gas alarm sounds. Someone strikes upon a shell-case, which usually hangs just outside a dug-out. We prefer the irritation of the gas to the extreme discomfort of the mask.

In this sector, we do two hours on guard, and have four hours off duty while in the front line. We lie down generally during the four hours. If we do not feel like sleeping, we write letters or play cards. Two men are always on guard at a time here. The enemy is not very many yards away from some of the posts.

At six o'clock one evening, two of us went on guard. The dug-out was only ten yards from the fire-step. It was, as usual, on the wrong side of the trench. Those whom we had relieved had just reached the mouth of the dug-out, when a trench-mortar shell landed right upon them. There was a roar and a shatter. None of us saw it coming; it happens like that sometimes. The bolt just comes out of the blue. There is nothing that one can do about it.

We hated occupying that post afterwards. The stains could be seen for weeks, and you never seemed to be able to lose the smell of the place. Even when back on rest, you could visualise the scene, and as you thought about it, a peculiar scent seemed to break in upon you. We did three more spells, each of two days, there. Each time became more hateful than the last. You just hoped that the same thing would not happen to you.

Another afternoon we were all cleaning ourselves near the same spot. The lice seemed to be more active than usual. Perhaps it was because the weather was getting warmer. We decided to ease ourselves. There is a limit to all things. So we took off our equipment and tunics and shirts.

At this point, the enemy was only twenty-five yards away. To undress in the front line is a great crime, but we knew that we were safe. Our new platoon officer only became a nuisance when we were back on rest. In this sector, we did not often see him. We only knew that he was alive because in the evenings the smell of steak and onions reached us. He would gorge himself in his dug-out, oblivious to everything except his own well-being.

We had not finished de-lousing ourselves when some trench-mortar shells began to come over a hundred yards down the trench. We could follow their flight from the time they were fired, and hear them hurtling through the air. Sergeant Waters was coming along to visit us, and we could see him in the distance. It was as dangerous to go back as it was to proceed. He came towards us. We told him when to run, and when to stop.

His chances of reaching us appeared to be twenty-to-one against. As we shouted, he took cover behind a traverse, and the trench-mortar landed in the next bay. We took on bets among ourselves as to whether he would reach us or not. In a few minutes he appeared round the corner where we were. He was breathless, and quite finished. We gave him a drink of rum. He was thoroughly liked by us all.

Fatigues involve all kinds of jobs in trench warfare. One night a section of our trench was blown in, and we had to re-make it before dawn. With picks, spades and sand-bags we started the job. Twenty men for forty yards. Before we had started our task, we were forced to leave it. The pick of one of the men struck something soft. It was moonlight; we were unearthing a corpse. He might have been German, English or French, as all these troops had occupied this part of the line.

Some of us are rapidly becoming nervous wrecks. There have been several cases of shell-shock, and of late, self-inflicted wounds have been common. There comes an end to all things. The human frame can only stand a certain amount. The nerves become terribly frayed.

We see the change taking place in each other, but say nothing. When a shell comes over, we duck. The daily machine-gunning, gas, trench-mortar shells, aerial bombing and gun-fire wear us out. We are forever trying to maintain life. But at any moment of the day or night the enemy might explode a mine beneath us. We live on the edge of a volcano. It is always active, and likely to erupt at any time.

I have seen as many as three a day go to the dressing-station voluntarily. Some would not return again to the trenches. It is better to lose a hand or foot, then lie out in the battlefield for hours or even days, with a gaping stomach wound.

I have seen men stand on the fire-step, and hold both arms above the parapet in the hope of getting hit. Sometimes their luck would be in, and a few of them have even got to England with as cushy wounds as they could have desired.

Shooting through a sack has been successful. A wet sack is generally chosen; the black powder sticks to it. At a distance of fifty yards, detection is difficult. Many cases have got away with it. But there are some things at which most of us draw the line. One of our men decided that he could stick it no longer. At the time, we were in a sap. He ripped open his trousers, and with a piece of rusty barbed wire he gashed himself deeply in the thigh. He tore at it to make the job complete, then he rubbed in a handful of foul earth. In a couple of days the thigh had swollen tremendously. It was double its normal size. It would certainly mean a court martial.

The hunt for souvenirs goes on. It is curious what a sense of values we have. In civilian life we would pass by a thing which attracts us in the trenches.

Very often when we are in the front-line trenches, one man goes out into No-man's-land or beyond. He never comes back empty-handed. He sometimes brings back stick-bombs; sometimes, little Jerry caps with bands of red, yellow or blue around them. An officer's revolver fetches a good price; he can often get fifty francs for one. If the price is low, he does not sell. He bides his time and holds on to his revolvers until the 'market' rises. The orderly room advises him when men are going home on leave.

He keeps these souvenirs in his pack, waiting for customers. He is also friendly with those in charge of the Battalion transport. Perhaps they go half-shares. It would be impossible for him to carry everything in his pack. You can always sell him a green envelope for a franc; he uses them to send home his winnings, because they are not opened by the censor.

We wonder when he will be captured. He seems to fear neither man nor devil. He takes part in every raid, and goes into German dug-outs. He is more keen on souvenirs than anything else, and he is the most foul-mouthed fellow I have ever known. His vocabulary is tremendously lewd.

There is another man who becomes rich too. But his exploits are less heroic. We do not admire him. He is a veritable Shylock, and never has anything to spare. No one has ever known him to give away even a cigarette. He is the Battalion barber. A hair-cut is one franc, and a shave is half a franc. If you do not tip him in advance, he will give you a prison cut. He also runs a 'crown and anchor' board. One week he sent four thousand francs to England. We have noticed that he does only one turn in the line out of four. Perhaps he is left out because of his age, or perhaps he finances somebody. It is difficult to get the truth always.

We have no love for those who fire trench-mortars, either the enemy or our own men. Our own artillery fellows come right into the front line carrying their 'Stokes' mortars. They send over a few shells from a certain point, and then move on. Those who are left to hold the line always know that this practice means trouble. The shelling is unmerciful at times, and in the forward posts there is not much good cover. We just stay like Aunt Sallies. It reminds me of a village fair, in which a man wearing a top hat walks behind some wire netting while the crowd knock off his hat with heavy wooden balls.

The enemy shell us as we go down the communication trench behind the tunnel. He must have spotted that a relief is in progress. We hurry on, but cannot go very fast. There are troops coming in, and you must always make way for them. The high explosives fall near us, with a noise like an electric train in an underground railway as it rips out of a station. The black smoke hangs over the trench.

Stretcher-bearers, at the double, come running up. They attend to the casualties. You make way for them too. Five minutes, or even one minute, may make all the difference to the wounded as they go to the dressing-station.

Some are killed before they reach the line; others as they leave it. Some who are now coming in have already been wounded two or even three times. Others are coming into the line for the first time.

We go back about five or six miles to the small town of Noeux-les-mines. There is a comfortable hut for each platoon. When we get there, we are dog-tired, and lie down on the bare planks. The blankets are already there. We sleep in our clothes, but that does not worry us in the least as we have done so for a long time.

Next morning breakfast is at nine o'clock. We line up with our mess tins and get some porridge. We also have bread and bacon and tea. The tea is far too sweet for my liking, but most of the troops seem to like it that way. After breakfast we shave and bath and clean our equipment. Buttons and badges are polished as in

England. We are at a loss to know the reason for this kind of thing. The next time up the line they will become dirty again. We do not know how this makes one a better soldier. But we are not supposed to think. Anyone who thinks can never become a good soldier. A good soldier is one who always does what he is told to do. In our school days we had been told that the power to think differentiated man from beast. In the army there are other rules, and a completely different sense of values. The 'other ranks' must be kept busy at any cost.

When we are clean, we are inspected. Our platoon officer is a fine barrack-square soldier. He stands nearly six feet, and throws his chest out well. He has a small moustache, a florid complexion, and is able to look fierce. His nightly supper of steak and onions agrees with him. He seems to have put on weight after every tour in the line. If any man at the Front can survive the war, he seems likely to be that person. He has brought the act of self-preservation to a fine art.

While back on rest he is everywhere at once. He wears a medal. We wonder how he came by it. He has been wounded once – in the back of the thigh. We do not think an enemy bullet could have caught him in the act of turning to encourage his men and leading them in an attack. The older hands wink knowingly when the subject is discussed. Perhaps they know more than they are willing to divulge.

There is no difficulty in passing the time. We are at rest, but every morning we parade and spend four hours monotonously. There is always Swedish drill and bayonet practice. We stretch our arms and legs and turn our heads to the right and left. We lie down quickly and get up quickly. We double march and slow march. We leap over trenches, and stab at large sacks full of straw. Some of them are suspended like a child's swing. Others lie flat on the ground. He who yells loudest is commended by the instructor.

Then follows Platoon and Company drill. We turn right-about and left-about. There comes the command 'Eyes-right', and we know we are passing some dignitary.

We know all about these things. When we were in training we learnt them, and we have done them over and over again a thousand times since. But in the army there are only a certain number of things to learn. After rifle and equipment and kit inspection, we have a lecture on the parts of a rifle, or on the causes of stoppages in Lewis guns. There are three kinds of stoppages: Class 1, Class 2, and Class 3. By elimination, we arrive at the probable cause of the stoppage. We can repeat the work just like the alphabet. The lecturer knows how sick we are of his words. If he is a decent fellow, he talks about other things and only remembers about the causes of the stoppage in a Lewis gun as the officer comes nearer to see if all goes well.

At dinner time we draw our rations. They consist of soup in which big lumps of fat swim about, and boiled rice containing figs. Every fourth day there is roast meat. Each company takes its turn. We think it is horse flesh, because it looks and tastes unlike the flesh of cattle. It is coarse-grained, pink in colour and leathery. But we welcome it because it is a change.

In the afternoons we have football matches. There are sports too, and Divisional Horse Shows. But these things are only for the well-behaved. All offenders stay behind in the camp. They pick up matches and cigarette ends around the officers' huts, or clean up the cooking utensils with sand. Some of them peel potatoes for the next day's dinner. The police sergeant is in charge of them. You cannot mistake him; he wears a band of red cloth around his arm, and always carries a swagger cane. All the provost sergeants look alike. They are always big and fat and brutal. They might have been turned out of a mould. They are an indispensable part of the Army, and much in evidence behind the line where they can really throw their weight about.

In the evenings, we have various ways of passing the time. Occasionally, a variety troupe gives a show. There is always a little conjuring, comic songs and community singing, and various forms of mimicry help to give us a smile.

CHAPTER SIX

Back on Rest

There isn't a single one of us who likes the Company Captain. Nobody can ever find a good word to say about this man. He is a small-minded and officious type. He is for ever sneering and snooping about when we are out of the line. There is a thoroughly nasty curl about his mouth which we dislike intensely. He is always particularly happy if he can take a rise out of someone, and the weaker his victim, the more he enjoys himself. How his wife must hate him! If the Colonel happens to be around, he becomes specially antagonistic and vociferous. A little power, albeit only temporary, has gone to his head. When we are in the line, he never comes anywhere near us. We don't know where he hides himself, nor what he does to pass the long days and nights.

Jones has a theory that he hates the lot of us because most of the men in the Company have had a far better education than he has had. Certainly his grammar is all upside-down and inside-out. He cannot even put the simplest sentence together properly. Jones is a pretty shrewd Lancastrian, and may not be wide of the mark in his guess. It would offer a reasonable explanation for his hostility to us.

If he knows one thing well it is how to look after his own skin.

Ours don't count for anything. If scheming can do it, he should manage to see the war out successfully, and emerge as quite a hero.

Casualties keep mounting up day by day. There is never anything spectacular; no long daily list, such as accompanies a very fierce battle, but there is a steady drain of up to a dozen and sometimes even more every day. Over a lengthy period the inroads become marked. Fresh drafts arrive fairly frequently to replace those who have been killed or wounded and sent down the line for treatment in hospital. They are nearly all caused by high-explosive shells and shrapnel, as the Hun gives us a dose of each of them every day. There is always one hand-out in the morning and another in the evening, and minenwerfers come hurtling through the air at irregular intervals for good measure.

As rocks will, in time, become eroded by falling water, so men's nerves become frayed from being too long in the line at a stretch. The last straw breaks the camel's back, and anything can happen to a man when he has to put up with the explosions of bursting shells, and the hideous sight of his best friend being dismembered. To these can be added confinement for weeks on end within a few yards, prolonged periods of sleeplessness, a monotonous and insufficient diet, and whatever inclement weather the gods may choose to send.

The top brass must know all about these matters, but they never have to experience them. This is where the rub lies. For them the war is a distant thing. For them it means a reasonably comfortable bed, early promotion, good rations, and plenty of whisky to wash them down. For them it means good company with whom to pass the idle hours, steady employment on good pay, and complete safety in heavily-guarded chateaux many miles behind the Front.

Time drags by. We can hardly wait for Monday to come, when

we are due to go back on rest, and are like schoolboys who have long looked forward to some exciting event, and fear that something may happen before the day comes. Some of us are little more than schoolboys, and this may be the reason for our impatience. Or it may be that we know that there will never be a Monday for some of us. When you are in the front line you can never take anything for granted. Before the next forty-eight hours have passed we might have to go out on a wiring or bombing raid. Or the Hun might decide to come over to us. Or the 5.9's might start falling among us and around us. We have become apprehensive, and live only a day at a time. For us there is never any tomorrow or the day after it. We cannot count on anything as a certainty any longer. There are too many disappointments when danger is omnipresent.

We have been relieved by the 16th Division who took over our posts in the Hohenzollern Sector. We tell them where the German line runs along our immediate front, and pass on any other bits of information that might be of use to them, such as taking cover at certain times each day when the shelling will begin. We warn them to keep an eye wide open for trench mortars as Jerry uses them freely here. He is so punctilious in all that he does that one can almost set one's watch by the morning and evening hymn of hate. His gunners are never two minutes out one way or the other. This is the Teutonic idea of efficiency. If they were to stagger their straffing, and by so doing catch us off our guard, they would reap a richer harvest.

We show the incoming troops where our dug-out is, and hand over all hand-grenades and spare ammunition. Those of us who have read our papers and magazines and books from home also pass them on. They will all help to while away off-duty hours, and take the thoughts of the men away from their environment, if only for brief periods.

When there is nothing else to be done, we make for the communication trench called Railway Alley and wend our way along it. It is slow going, as the trench is crowded. Fritz is aware that a relief is in progress. Observers in the long sausage balloons high up and behind his lines have spotted much more than the normal coming and going up to the Front, and signalled this information to the artillery. How we wish that our airmen would attack these balloons and send them down in flames! If they did so it would save many lives. There are few things that cheer the foot-sloggers up so much as to see these sky-look-out-men hurrying to earth, in what appear to be little bucket seats at the end of a long tether, while the fabric of their balloons burns furiously above them.

The whizz-bangs go screaming and whistling past us. They are immediately overhead, and burst with a sharp crack just beyond us. But we are seven feet below the surface, and know that these daisy-cutters cannot harm us unless they hit the side of the trench or explode right over us. The coal-boxes are a different kettle of fish, as they come straight down and shatter everything around on strking the ground. Then there is a blinding flash and a roar.

The enemy gunners have our range. Shells seem to pursue us as we hurry along. There is no safety anywhere until we get out of the range of the guns. Some of our men have no luck. A few yards behind us someone calls out 'Stretcher-bearer! At the double!' We make way for them, but nobody can move quickly through the two-way traffic.

Five men have been killed and eight others wounded by a single shell. Three of the wounded will never reach the dressing-station alive. No power on earth can help them. One has lost both his legs. Another has been hit in the chest, and his right arm is almost cut off near the shoulder. The third one has extensive head wounds. The lower half of his face has been blown away. The cries are quite pitiful, and unnerving to us all.

Less than an hour ago we were all together in the front line and making plans for passing the time when back on rest. If we had remained there, this would never have happened. If we had been five minutes earlier or later in leaving, it would have made all the difference. But who was to know these things? If Jerry had dropped the shell a little farther on or a bit shorter, the dead and the wounded would still be with us. If they had even been around another traverse, they would have escaped uninjured. But there are so many 'ifs' that come into our lives in the trenches that we have come to realise that any amount of planning is quite useless. As often as not, rational thinking will get us nowhere. Perhaps the soldier more than any other man believes that

'There's a divinity that shapes our ends,
'Rough-hew them how we will.'

There is still half a mile to go before we reach the end of the communication trench. We can see the big shells falling around us. Columns of thick black smoke mushroom upwards as each shell bursts with a terrifying roar. The fumes nearly choke us. We cough and splutter, and spit out thick dust mixed with lots of saliva. 'Stretcher-bearers!' Again the shout is heard. Again we press ourselves back to let them get as quickly as possible to those who need their help. Two of them will not require any assistance. They can be left until things quieten down a bit, and then be removed for burial. Four more wounded can perhaps be patched up. Two of them are able to walk. One has been hit in the shoulder, and the other holds up a mutilated left hand.

The walking wounded are the fortunate ones. We wish them luck as they file past us, and would gladly change places with them. They won't be back in the line again for several months, and if fortune smiles upon them they might even get to Blighty. We know that when they return to the Battalion, if they ever do, some of us may not be here to welcome them back. They are more sure of what the future has in store for them than we are. They will soon be able to sleep between clean sheets, while the lice are worrying the life out of us. They will be certain of three well-cooked meals every day, while we go hungry if anything should happen to prevent the ration party from reaching us. However irksome hospital routine may be for them, they will get a smile and an encouraging word from the doctors and nurses to keep them going, while we shall be subjected to sarcasm and sneers, and harried from pillar to post by our Company Commander.

At length we come to the end of the communication trench and are able to disperse. Little groups fan out to left and right. It is safer that way, as the target becomes smaller and less definite. But a well-directed shell or even a stray one can still catch us as we come out into the open countryside. Our destination is Noeux--les-mines about five miles away. This is coal-mining country, and an enormous black slag heap lies near the camp to which we are going. In this part of France there are coal mines and slag heaps every few miles. We have been assured of a hot meal on arrival. Our Battalion cooks always come up to scratch, and we can rely on them to give of their best. Back on rest, a hot meal is invariably smoking hot, and our portions are liberal.

We are allotted accommodation on arrival at our destination, and move into a large rectangular wooden hut with a corrugated iron roof. There are many of these huts, and each will hold forty men. Every hut has an NCO – a sergeant or corporal in charge. All who go into or out of the camp must pass through a gateway. There is a sentry box just inside it.

Our beds consist of four flooring boards resting on low trestles. We are six inches off the wooden floor, and have three blankets apiece. One serves as an under-blanket. Overcoats can be used to supplement the two which cover us, or by drawing two beds together one can share four blankets with one's half-section.

Nobody will ever be persuaded to team up with B—. He wets his bed every night. One of the sentries has orders to awaken him in the night, but even this arrangement does not achieve its purpose. The poor fellow simply cannot help himself. He has always been like this, and should never have been passed as fit by the medical officer. There is frequently a puddle under his bed in the morning. Everybody fights shy of being near him. The plain truth is that he smells of stale urine all the time.

B— will never make a soldier. He will never make anything. He is sloppy – just a large hunk of flesh. He cannot throw a hand-grenade any distance. He is a menace to everybody near him when he picks up a loaded rifle. A bayonet thrust is quite beyond his understanding. A long jab and a short jab are the same thing to him, and he is the despair of the physical jerks instructor.

H— is another of the world's unfortunates, and a liability. He is slow of speech, and has the vocabulary of an eight-year-old child. His lower lip droops, and he dribbles incessantly. He is simple-minded but quite harmless. He will never be able to fend for himself in this world. Like B—, he should never have been drafted into an active-service battalion. He will never kill a German, and is useless in the line. He hasn't got a real friend, but many in the platoon are kind to him.

O— is the third dud in the Company. He is big and powerful, but mentally weak. As a navvy doing pick and shovel work, he can hold his own; but when it comes to thinking and reasoning he is lost. He is a bad-tempered fellow, and not very advanced in the animal kingdom. In some respects he is not unlike a gorilla. His speech is incoherent, and he takes offence easily. He is a lone wolf, and more to the pitied than blamed.

'We shield these three members of our Company as much as possible; but the Captain appears to enjoy being bestial to them. They cannot hit back at him, and are like sheep before their shearer.

We line up for dinner and receive a large slice of bread, a piece of meat as big as a man's hand, a potato and lashings of appetising gravy. The meat is hard and tough and close-grained. We think it is horse meat. But it is a change from the everlasting bully, and we manage to eat it. The bread is really first-class, and as good as any of us has ever had in civilian life. Bread is something that comes up from the Base. The bakers there really know their job, and have never been known to let us down.

For 'afters' – the second course – there is boiled rice with sultanas in it. This is a bit of a mess, but it is satisfying, and a change of diet. In the line there is never any second helping. There is a canteen in the reserve or third line where one can buy biscuits, but our pay doesn't run to that except for special occasions.

The Fritzes think that we live like kings. They envy us our bully beef and white bread. Their very dark-brown rye bread, sauerkraut and sausage of doubtful ancestry would not appeal to us. We should starve like rats on their rations.

The rest of the working day is spent cleaning up. We begin by drawing our packs from a store-room, and then go to a communal wash-house. Hot water is available, and there are simple but efficient sprinklers. We have to queue for them, but cannot stay here as long as we would wish, for hundreds of men are awaiting their turn.

Then we go back to our hut and the spit and polish. From our packs we take out button-sticks, polish, cloths and brushes. Hat badges, shoulder brassware, tunic buttons, webbing equipment and boots must all be attended to, and our clothing must show no sign of mud or dust. Then our rifles must be cleaned and oiled. A dirty barrel will mean at least the loss of freedom in off-duty time for four days. It might even mean pack drill on the parade ground.

This cleaning-up game is supposed to be good for our morale. Perhaps it is. It would be so easy to start sliding downhill, and we should then look no better than Falstaff's ragamuffins.

We call the next day 'lining-up day'. It begins with four men at a time sweeping out the hut. We shall all take our turn at doing this work. Then the beds are arranged neatly in line. They must not be even half-an-inch out. The Army loves straight lines. Blankets have all to be folded in a certain manner, and any deviation is never tolerated. We work by the clock, and in due course the Orderly Officer appears. Every man stands to attention beside his bed, with thumbs in line with the seams of his trousers. The great man is accompanied by an NCO. 'Take his name!' he says, if anyone has folded his blankets wrongly, or placed them untidily on the planks. In due course the offender will appear before his betters.

The next line-up parade is for kit inspection. We lay out all our possessions on our beds. Vests, shirts, underpants, socks, razor and everything else that has been issued must all be on view. Even the little cloth 'housewife' which contains mending things like thread and needles must be laid out. If anything is missing, the careless person will be in trouble and charged for every replacement.

Then the Company Captain has his turn. We line up wearing our equipment, and with our rifles on our shoulders. Bolts are removed from the rifles. If a man has not shaved, or if his puttees are wrongly wound, or his equipment has been insufficiently attended to, or his clothing is spotted, however slightly, he will be for the high jump.

We are inspected from front and rear. 'Hair-cut!' says the officer. 'And you! And you! And you!' he says, tapping each man on the back as he moves along the ranks.

Not every rifle is examined, but you can never take a chance. To have an unclean rifle is a crime of a very serious nature. Our Captain almost explodes if he sees a speck of dust in the barrel. There are never any extenuating circumstances. Black is black and white is white. That is something which he understands. He glares and fumes, and looks as if he might have a stroke if there is the slightest sign of rust. 'Take his name!' he barks to the Sergeant who accompanies him on his inspection. He almost screams the words out.

He suffers from a permanent disadvantage in that he is only five feet seven in height. This might account for his inferiority complex and aggressiveness. He must assert his authority over us in some way, and bullying is the way he chooses. This makes him feel that he has the edge on us. It atones for his lack of inches.

The last line-up for the day is the pay parade. The Captain glares at us as we draw near. If it were possible, he would deprive us all of our cash. Clearly, he doesn't think that we have earned it, and therefore have no right to it. We have other ideas. A foreigner might think that he was dispensing alms to beggars.

The surly O— is just ahead of me. He is in trouble from the moment he begins to move. His gait is awkward, and his reactions are always slow. He comes to the salute, but it is not good enough. There is nothing that he can do properly when he has to act on his own, and he looks bewildered as his right arm drops limply to his side. The Captain storms at him. 'Don't you know how to salute?' he asks. Sergeant Waters is standing near the table, and to him the Captain says, 'Give this man an hour's saluting drill'.

We are sorry for O—. He has done his best. But we also feel that our Company Commander has a case. O— would try the patience of Job. Sergeant Waters has a very kind heart, and will attend to the matter in his own way. The offender will be let off lightly by this very gentle man. In our platoon he is always called 'Polly'; I do not know the reason for this nickname. He knows that O— will never be of use to anybody, and he will be very kind to him.

We decide to spend the evening in town. It is a one-horse place. There appears to be only a single street. Three estaminets are open. With so many troops about, they are all doing good business. If the war has brought inconveniences, there are compensations that probably outweigh them. Nobody knows better than the French people how to improve the shining hour, and this is their big chance. They grasp it with both hands, and will emerge with what is to them great wealth.

There are six of us, and we are feeling affluent. Forbes suggests that we have eggs and chips every evening while we have the chance. Such a feast doesn't often come our way. We all know that the next time in the line might be the last for us, and then some others will inherit our wealth. We have seen this happen to others who have put a little away just to be on the safe side. There is never any safe side for us. We have become realists. We walk up and down the street searching for some place where we can spend the evening. Only the best will do. Finally, we decide upon one and knock on the door. Madame will be very pleased to attend to us. We follow her in and make ourselves at home. This is comfort such as we have not known for a long time, and we decide to make the most of it. 'If only we could have this for ever, I'd stay in the Army for the rest of my life', says Moore.

A plate of chips, an egg, a slice of bread and a glass of vin rouge costs us three francs. This is almost three and a half days' pay, but we don't mind that. It is money well spent. It is not often that we treat ourselves in this way.

Encore, Madame, s'il vous plaît' I say to the lady of the house.

She smiles. *'C'est un plaisir'*, she replies, and hurries off to repeat the order.

In ten minutes our second helping is on the table. Sinclair looks at his plate as though he could go on eating for the rest of the evening. He is a Scot, and the son of a crofter. Life has never been easy for him, and this is luxury indeed.

We are not in a hurry, and after half-an-hour decide to have a third round. This should see us through for the evening. Even the best of times must come to an end.

When half-past nine approaches, we thank Madame for her hospitality and tell her that we shall be coming back to-morrow. She beams upon us, and sees us out in a polite manner.

The next day begins with physical training. Our instructor is a jack-in-the-box, Sergeant Dalrymple. He looks as though he is made of india-rubber, and is terribly efficient. We stretch and bend in all directions, and do push-ups by the dozen. Hickey, Boucher and Oldfield are in the awkward squad, and come in for special attention while the rest of us stand easy. But no talking is permitted.

The sergeant is relentless and keeps the inefficient ones on their toes. They sweat and look daggers at their persecutor, but are powerless. This is the price they have to pay for having been born stupid.

Sergeant Waters is more understanding. When the platoon officer tells him to give us a lecture on the parts of a rifle, he marches our squad to a quiet part of the field.

'You fellows don't want to hear anything more about the make-up of the ruddy thing', he says. 'You've all stripped your rifles a hundred times already, and know as much as I do about it.'

The Battalion falls in for a route march. All the senior officers mount their horses. Passing through the town our rifles are at the slope, but when the long column is clear of it, we march at ease. At the end of an hour we halt and fall out for ten minutes' rest. Off comes our harness. We stretch out by a hedgerow and pipes and cigarettes are lit.

The next stopping place is beside a large wood. It is near Barlin. We are due to spend the night here, and set up bivouacs to give us shelter. Groundsheets are slung between the trees. Bracken makes a delightful mattress. Birds sing all around us. Not far away from where we lie, someone produces a mouth organ. He is an expert, and entertains us for an hour or more with classical music and popular melodies. At times the wood rings as we all burst into song. If anything can make us forget our worries, this is it.

Field cooks prepare our food, and a late supper of tea and army biscuits or scalding soup is even laid on. It is not often that we have a choice of food. Our prize scrounger manages to get two helpings of soup, and follows this up with a large sandwich of bread and cheese. He is first class at getting on the right side of the sergeant cook. His capacity for food is limitless. Long after the rest of us have finished eating, he goes on and on. This is not because he eats slowly; in fact he wolfs his food down.

The mouth organ bursts forth again. Hundreds of voices join in singing songs of home. 'Blighty' is one of them. Physically, we are in the wood, but in spirit we are very far away. Then a man with a good tenor voice takes over, and we listen to his rendering of 'Mountain Lovers' and 'If you were the only girl in the world' and 'There's a long, long, trail a-winding'.

The stars come out, and we settle down for the night. But before we can get to sleep, we hear the sound of engines overhead. The German airmen are on their way to our rear to bomb some airfield or supply dump. In half-and-hour they are back. There are close on a thousand men in the wood beneath them. What a target we would be! The deep rhythmic sound of the efficient engines grows more faint. We turn over in our silvan haven, and know no more until the bugle calls us to show a leg.

One day passes into another. We have Company drill. We form fours, turn to the right and left, and about-turn as though this was our first day on the parade ground. Then follows rifle drill by numbers. One man faints and flops to the ground. His rifle makes a clatter and this angers our Company Captain. Perhaps he thinks that no man in one of the best divisions of the British Army has the right to faint, and that we should all be made of sterner stuff. Sergeant Waters attends to the prostrate man. He handles him gently, and leads him away when he has recovered. It is little acts like this that have endeared Polly to us. None of us has ever known him do an unkind act to anybody.

The last day is devoted to lectures. One is on gas, and we learn all over again how to adjust our masks. Another lecture is on personal hygiene when in the line. As there is never any water to spare there, we fail to see how we can practise what the lecturer preaches. We ask him how to control the omnivorous lice which worry us by day and by night. He cannot answer that one.

'It's a matter of personal hygiene', he says.

'But the cleanest among us are no better off than anybody else,' we say.

This causes him to turn away. He gives us up as unpromising material. His next audience may be more amenable, and give him a better hearing.

CHAPTER SEVEN

C'est La Guerre

From near Barlin we have travelled in buses to Tangry, a village many miles behind the Front. The people here appear to be oblivious to the fact that there is a war on. They lead normal lives and there is no shortage of food. Our billet is a cowshed. We see a great deal of the country and love it because we are not accustomed to crops and flowers. Where we have come from we saw only red poppies growing. We wish that we could end our days in this Elysium. But after a few days here we move on again.

We march to Pernes and entrain for Arras. Our Division is now attached to the Canadian Corps. As we go into the city early the next morning, it looks as if it has been wrecked by an earthquake. There are some houses still intact, but they are not numerous. Whole streets have been flattened by the German bombs and shells. Soldiers come out of cellars and even the most ruined-looking places. There are thousands of troops here.

The railway station has been destroyed. It had a glass roof, but now the glass is nearly all gone. The steel framework still holds in places, but large strips of metal hang down to the ground. On the rails there is a huge fifteen-inch gun. The Germans also have one behind their lines. We call it 'Perishing Percy'.

From Arras we march to Achicourt and spend the night there.

The next day we take up positions in the trenches at Wancourt. It is a desolate place. In the evening we move forward. A well-defined road runs toward the enemy lines. It is a brilliant moonlight night, and we can see the road running far ahead.

The road is blocked with troops and horse transport. There are field guns and ammunition lumbers by the score. Field-kitchens rattle along. Red Cross wagons hurry past. They are all going forward to take part in the attack tomorrow. All is bustle and noise.

Suddenly we hear the sound of aeroplane engines. They are not flying high. They come nearer. We can tell they are enemy planes, as their engines make a deeper-pitched noise than our own. This can only mean one thing. The enemy has knowledge of the impending attack, and he knows that the back areas will be as busy as ant-hills. There will be life everywhere, and the roads good targets on moonlight nights.

The planes come lower, and fly along the road. With a deafening noise a bomb bursts. Others follow. The road which was alive becomes a place of death. The riders and the drivers curse; they can do nothing but go forward. A hole in the road holds up the transport. So does a heap of wounded and dead animals and men.

The traffic accumulates at such a spot, and the enemy flies back again bombing and machine-gunning. The horses scream with terror. The drivers try to extricate themselves. Those who are near to the side of the road get off into a ditch or anywhere else that is possible. One thinks only of escape.

We scatter as much as we can. The infantry run like frightened rabbits. It is not often that they feel that they have an advantage over the other troops. We lie flat on the grass. There is no cover, but at least we are off the road. We hear the swish, swish of the bombs as they cut through the air. Then comes a terrific crash. Even if one falls a hundred yards away, you think it is going to fall upon you.

Everything that is wounded, screams. The night is full of screaming. You know only two things; one is that you still live; the second is that all around you, stark naked tragedy is taking place. There are few things so piercing and sad as the scream of a terrified horse.

The bombing and the machine-gunning die down. The roar of the engines becomes fainter. They have used all their ammunition, and are returning home. They have done a good night's work. And many Iron Crosses will be given for it.

We realise, of course, that this kind of thing is by no means confined to one side. As the French people say, with a shrug of the shoulders, *'C'ést la guerre'*.

We move into the road again. Someone shouts the name of our regiment, and we come together once more. We have some distance still to go, and must be moving on again.

The Red Cross units attend to those who require help. Those who will never again need assistance are carried to one side of the road, or to the other side. The road is cleared.

As we go forward, we see the damage that has been done. Here are a dozen men. Half-an-hour ago, they were alive and moving into action. Odd ones and groups of half-a-dozen lie about. One looks at them in passing. One cannot count them. For a mile or more one can see them. 'Killed in action' is how they will be listed. Many buff-coloured envelopes will be delivered within the next few days. Many homes will be the poorer. Many heroes have gone on into eternity before their time.

Horses and half-horses litter the roadside. We pass close to one that has not been moved away. It is not so much mangled as the others. Its four legs stick up in mute appeal. The hooves have been blown clean off. Nothing else appears to have happened. It is dead. Half-an-hour ago it was probably a noble animal. Half-an-hour ago, someone cared for it. Now, it is worthless and cast away.

We think that soon, we will all be worthless and cast away. But at present we know that we still live. Our luck has held once more. But it cannot go on for ever.

Time passes. We halt at 3 a.m. close to some gun positions. They are sixty-pounders, and are just off the road. Beside them are huge stacks of shells. The muzzles of the guns are elevated to an angle of 50 degrees. They appear to be ready for their work. The men who will serve them are all busy. We can see the lights of their torches, even in the moonlight. Perhaps they are checking their angles and directions.

The howitzers are farther forward than usual. They are only a mile behind the jumping-off positions of the infantry. Clearly, much is expected from the impending action.

We are not the attacking troops this time. Our work is to act as 'moppers-up'. That is,we shall not take part in the main attack, unless we are needed. If the attack is held up, then our turn will come. Otherwise, we shall follow-up, and consolidate the positions won. In any case, we shall soon be in the front-line trenches, to relieve those who survive the attack.

Before daylight, the barrage begins. A gun on the right barks out. In a second, the Front leaps into flame as far as we can see to the left and to the right. It must be twelve to fifteen miles in all. The night has gone. The flame is continuous. It does not even flicker. I have never seen a greater concentration of guns. The Boches are really at the receiving end this time. They are getting a terrible hammering.

The number of shells sent over is simply colossal. They fall upon the enemy's line. You can see them burst. As dawn comes, the forward trenches are seen to be wrapped in smoke.

The eighteen-pounders in front of us fire over open sights. They are only a quarter of a mile behind the line. The heavies scream as they go along overhead. The whole of the Boches' front is aflame.

They are really having hell knocked out of them. Our gunners are really excelling themselves.

At six o'clock the guns fire more quickly. For fifteen minutes there is drum-fire. It is pandemonium. You almost feel a sense of pity for those upon whom the shells are falling. Those who escape death may live in mental anguish for the remainder of their lives. You know that they can never be normal men again.

For a moment, the rapid-firing ceases . . . The guns are increasing their range. The infantry are in the thick of the attack. As they get out of their trench and go across No-man's land, the barrage protects them. But it cannot protect all of them. We wonder if the attack is being successful, or if it is being held up. It means much to us, as we shall have to repeat it if it does not succeed.

In a few minutes we see men walking back from the front line. We cannot tell at first whether they are our own men or the enemy. Soon they come nearer. We see that some of them are in khaki, and some are in a field-grey uniform. Some are walking cases; others are carried. The stretcher-bearers are prisoners. They carry our badly wounded men.

Then come large groups of men. They wear little round hats. Fifty or a hundred pass us at a time. Two or three of our men take them to the rear. They look more like ghosts than human beings. They are ashen in colour. They have passed through hell. Some of them have not shaved for many days. In their huge boots they look terribly awkward.

We are sorry for them, and we stop them and give them cigarettes. They look grateful, but many of them cannot say a word. They just look at us. Their eyes are protruding. Their expressions are of horror and terror. You feel that if you shouted at them, they would jump with fear.

Some of them cannot light their cigarettes, and so we strike the matches and hold the cigarettes steady. They look gratefully at us and nod their heads. We have no common language, yet we have some things in common. Today it is their turn. Tomorrow it will be ours.

Before they move on again, one of them says to us, 'You English, you do not know a bombardment.' We know that he refers to the barrage of a few hours ago. He is one of those for whom we felt pity.

They move back to the cages prepared for them. They know that they will not again have the experience of the last few hours. The war is finished, so far as they are concerned. They still live; their chances of continuing to live are good. They are better than ours.

We move forward. The road has been almost destroyed. We open out into diamond formation, to offer smaller targets. Just to the right of us, behind the hill, is a squadron of cavalry. They have been there since dawn. There are also many horse-drawn vehicles of different kinds. An enemy plane comes over. It drops a flare. His artillery fires upon the cavalry and the hillside erupts and stampedes.

The shells fall among the horses. They are terribly frightened. They bolt in all directions, most of them unattended. They fall by the score. Their screams are heard for miles. Teams of six, pulling a field gun, and a pair pulling a limber, run down the hillside. They run madly. They cannot go far. They overturn, and the horses struggle until they can be released. Others have been hit, and their entrails hang out. They are wild with fear and pain. Their speed quickly slackens and they drop from sheer exhaustion.

In five minutes the shelling ceases. The hillside sickens us and we do not even look at it again. One must become callous in order that we may carry on.

As we go on, we pass our field-guns. They are still firing. The Front is entirely hidden in smoke. It hangs close to the ground and we cannot see anything beyond it. The shells must be falling upon the enemy's second or third line. We duck involuntarily as they go over our heads. They are not far above us.

In a few more minutes we come to our old front line.It is the trench from which the attack has been made. We jump into it, then over it. It is not badly knocked about, and so we think that our own troops have not been heavily shelled.

When we advance towards the enemy front line, we see many men lying about. They have been mown down by machine-gun fire. Some lie flat on their backs. Some are in a crouching position. Some grip a limb or press upon some part of the body. You do not need to look twice to see that they are dead. On some faces there is peace. On others there are signs of agony. Beside them lie their rifles. The bayonets are fixed, and gleam in the sunshine.

We pick up the rifles and stick them upright in the ground. The foot-long bayonets support the weight. It will be easy for those who clear up the battlefield to find the dead.

We pass a kilted soldier who is lying in a shell-hole. The colours of his kilt are easy to see. It is not a new shell-hole. You can tell that it is months old. In passing, we think that he has sought the friendly cover of this hole in the ground in which to bind up his wounds. But the flow of blood must have been too rapid for him to stop. A soaking-wet patch of earth beside him tells how he died.

Soon, we come to the first enemy trench. It is a strong point, and a tremendous amount of barbed wire lies all about it. It has been well cut up by our artillery fire. One can easily pass between the ends of it. The trench itself is a terrible thing to look at. It has been heavily attacked and stoutly defended. We can see fifty yards to the right and nearly as far to the left. Then it bends and we cannot look into it.

It is full to overflowing. It is six feet wide, and it must have been equally as deep. Now it is filled. There are German and Canadian and Scottish troops. We know them by their different uniforms.

The trench runs red. There are corpses and limbs everywhere. They are the price which Europe has paid for a hundred yards of ground.

Nearby, there stand eight machine-guns and five trench-mortars. Belts full of ammunition, and empty belts too, lie everywhere. The ground is strewn with them. Two or three German carts are nearby. They have large red crosses painted on a white background on their sides.

The resistance at this point must have been terrific. But even more so must have been the onslaught. Now, friend and foe lie together. It will be easy to bury them. The trench will just be covered in. It is the only thing to do. Hundreds of bodies are dismembered. You could not possibly sort them out.

A hundred deeds of valour will go unrewarded. A thousand names will be crossed off the register. An epic, greater than any of those of old, will never be told.

The attack has succeeded and we have advanced more than two miles. The casualties on our side have not been excessive.

We are not needed immediately in the front line, so we help to clear up the battlefield. Besides those who have just fallen, there are many of the enemy who have been lying out for days or even weeks. There has not been time to spare for them. Jerry is usually careful about burying his dead. Recently he must have been too much occupied with strengthening his defences to meet the attack.

With picks and spades we make a huge hole by connecting the existing shell-holes. It is many feet deep and roughly rectangular. Thirty yards by twenty is the size of it. Then we spread out, and call to one another as we come across a corpse. It is disgusting work, but it must be done. The pioneers will have plenty to do before the week is finished.

We carry some, and we roll others along the ground. You could not possibly carry them. We have tried to do so, but have not been successful. An arm or a leg or even a couple of limbs have come away in our hands. If we find a waterproof sheet, we use it. It is a little more humane to do so. Then four of us carry the ground-sheet to the hole we have made. We tip out our load, then search again. It is a long job, and heavy work. Myriads of flies buzz round. They do not go far away. They do not make any distinctions between the German dead and our own. All corpses are grist to their mill.

Three times we have had to stop and run for cover. An observation balloon, far ahead of us, has spotted us. Perhaps they do not know what we are doing. Or perhaps they do. In any case, it makes no difference. We offer a good target. The shells land close to us. Four of our men are wounded. Two of them are lucky; one is hit above the elbow, and the second gets it in the fleshy part of the thigh. They could not wish for cleaner wounds. As we say goodbye to them, they are quite cheerful. They wish us luck as we get them ready to go back. We envy them, and we tell them so.

The other two are serious cases. Head wounds are always dangerous. We put on some iodine, then bandage them up and send them on stretchers to the dressing-station.

Each time we return to collect the dead, we are fired at, and so we decide to finish the task later when observation will not be possible. We come upon a dug-out. It is deep and perfectly safe, so we decide to spend the night in it. It is dark thirty steps down, and we light a candle. By its flickering light we see three field-grey uniforms. But these men are harmless. Our men must have bombed them in passing over. It is a common practice, and both sides do it. It saves time and trouble, and is always final.

They cannot do us any harm, so we roll them to one side of the dug-out and leave them there. Then we settle down for the night, and in a few minutes we are mostly asleep.

Before the candle quite burns itself out, I settle down to write a letter. It is many days since I have written home, and they will be getting anxious about me. There may be no time tomorrow, as it is certain that the attack will be continued with the return of daylight.

An hour before dawn we 'stand-to' as this is the time when things happen quickly. With the first streak of daylight,we notice that our own observation balloons are up. We can see at least eight of them along the line.

Suddenly we hear the noise of an aeroplane. Then follows the rat-tat-tat of a machine-gun. One of the balloons bursts into flames. Within two minutes two of the others have been set on fire. The observers come to earth in their parachutes.

We have come into Cachencourt Wood. Many of the enemy sheltered here. They lie about thickly. It may be that they had run here for cover, or perhaps a Company assembled to make a counter-attack. They are mostly middle-aged men. There are not many who are under forty years of age. Their wives will think of them as having died like heroes. Their children will know them no more. They will remember them because they died in defence of the Fatherland. They will be told the same old story, and they will believe it. *Dulce et decorum est pro patria mori.*

We have heard the same story, but we do not believe it. At one time we were deceived just like the rest. But now we see through their lies. A little experience soon teaches one many things.

These men interest us because we have not seen anybody like them before. Some of them still wear their steel helmets which come well down below their ears. Many still have on the little peculiar round hats which we have collected as souvenirs in the past. There is a red band around these hats, and on some of them a number of small buttons. A few have no hat on. Their hair is always cropped close.

All these men have turned blue-black in colour. They have only been dead one day, and at first their appearance is a little terrifying. We inspect them closely, and decide that they have been gassed.

On previous occasions, gas has been sent over from trenches occupied by us. Only a month ago, four hundred drums were sent across No-man's-land in our sector. But we have not previously been able to follow up and see the result.

We do not know if this is chlorine or phosgene, or some more deadly gas than either of them. Whatever kind of gas it may be, it is clearly terribly lethal.

Squeamishness has no place in our lives. If it had,we should fare badly. So it matters little to us that the enemy lie about us. We very soon forget all about them, and cease to look at them. We are only reminded of them when the humorist of our party throws a crust to one of them and says, 'Take that, Jerry!'

We laugh because we think it is a good joke. Before we have finished laughing, we think how times have changed. In civilian life we should never dream of laughing at such an incident. The incident itself would not be possible, to begin with, and we should ostracise anyone who dreamed of making fun out of tragedy. We have changed too.

Some of us realise that it is not our real selves who laugh. Something other than our real selves has taken possession of us for the time being. It is a form of self-preservation that is at work within us. Perhaps we are not entirely responsible. We may not even be responsible at all. Almost every day we see things that must make the angels weep. And if we laugh, it is that we may not weep too. We can only maintain life by laughing at the wrong times and in the wrong places.

We know that the times are out of joint, and perhaps they will not be put right again while we live.

Five miles ahead, and to the left of us, is an attractive-looking town. The houses appear to be colour-washed on the outside. We can see them clearly against a green background. The roofs are of red tiles. The town scintillates in the afternoon sunshine.

The enemy must have had very comfortable billets in this town. It has not been knocked about at all. The inhabitants have continued to live there all the time the war has been on.

In the evening, we move on again to relieve those who are in the line. The Second Battle of Arras has died down. We have advanced more than three miles. Eight thousand prisoners have been taken. A large number of trench-mortars and machine-guns have been captured. Some field-guns have fallen into our hands, and a number of them have been turned upon the enemy.

We remain four more days in the line, and consolidate it. The enemy, though vigilant, does not disturb us. He has been too much shaken by the attacks of the Scottish and Canadian troops, and the drubbing which he has received from our artillery.

CHAPTER EIGHT

Good-Bye Polly

Our Division is to go southward to the Somme region, and we think that we shall soon be for the high jump. The British troops there are attacking the Germans heavily. The enemy is offering a stubborn resistance, and much fierce fighting is taking place along a wide front.

We leave our position to the east of Vis-en-Artois where we have helped to drive the Jerries out of the line, and go back to Aubigny. There we climb up into cattle trucks which carry either ten horses or forty men. We go lumbering along until we reach St Pol where the train stops. Some of us get out to stretch our legs, and we are told that we shall be here for three hours. We are hungry, and one man who has been here before says that he knows a place where we can get a good square meal. Four of us go down into the town. We have hardly finished eating when we hear a train whistling. We pay our bill and hurry back to the station, but find that our train has gone.

The RTO says that he will do his best for us, and tells us to see him in the morning. After spending the night at the station, we seek him out. He recognises us, and gives us a note for our Company Captain. In it he explains why we missed the train, and says that we are being sent on to our unit by the first available train. It takes us to the city of Amiens. Then we go a few miles to Villers-Bretonneux and find that our Battalion is billeted there in ruined houses. There is hardly anything left of the town which nestles in a hollow. In some of the streets there are shallow trenches. Only twenty yards separated the Jerries and the Aussies.

The fighting here must have been desperately fierce, and often hand-to-hand. This was the farthest point reached by the advancing German army in their drive for Amiens. It was here that they attacked in hordes and were mown down. As one wave faltered or fell back, another took its place. It was here that the men from the Never-Never fought with their backs to the wall and barred the way and flung the Germans back. There are no finer fighting men than the Australians. The Huns really fear them.

Just outside the town are huge piles of British and German rifles, leather and webbing equipment, ammunition and clothing. Everything has been picked up on the battlefield.

Along the rising ground to the east of the town there are several lines of trenches where the Germans dug themselves in, in their attempt to stabilise the line. But the Aussies drove them out of these positions and then over the crest of the hill and many miles beyond it.

The next morning we parade, and have our supply of iron rations made good. Two ounces of tea, a tin of corned beef and a few hard biscuits are issued to each man. We hand in our overcoats, blankets and packs, but keep our haversacks. Then follows rifle, bayonet, equipment and ammunition inspection. One hundred and twenty rounds of live ammunition is what we carry. Rusty clips are exchanged for fresh ones as they hinder the rapidity of loading. We can put three clips into out magazines at a time. Our rifles are really miniature machine-guns. Fifteen rounds a minute are calculated to make a man keep his head down, as we can fire from the hip when advancing.

We exchange all our American ammunition for British-made. It has been said, though we do not know with what truth, that it is partly filled with cardboard, and therefore much less effective. Nothing but the best will do for us, as the only good German is a dead one. So we cannot afford to take chances.

When all is ready, we move up to the line again. We board the London buses which are waiting in the road. Some of them still have their numbers on them. One is a 77. Perhaps this very bus once took me down to the Surrey woods in bluebell time. It all comes back so clearly. I would get off it at Sutton, and make my way into the woods from there in search of bluebells, honeysuckle and nightingales' nests.

Others buses carry signs such as Pimlico, Marylebone and Aldwych. They have all done yeoman service, and transported troops from Ypres to St. Quentin and from Arras to Armentières.

We climb upstairs as usual, and secure a front seat from force of habit. It is the vantage point and we are reminded of the days long past when we went sight-seeing in London. For some of us this will be the last journey we shall make. We know that the enemy is putting up a stern resistance, and that stiff work lies ahead of us. He has retired to his much-vaunted lines of defence. They are said to be impregnable, and it is our business to drive him out of them. The newspapers at home will soon have many columns of the casualties every day. Some of us will be listed there.

The long straight road is known to some of us, as we were here many months ago under other conditions. Since that time, the tide of battle has rolled twice along it; once backward, and then forward again.

We drive for some hours. On the right and on the left there is nothing but destruction. Trees have been felled for purposes of obstruction and to prevent observation of movements. In places the road has been blown up. The drivers can scarcely creep past the holes. The buses lurch over, and we incline our bodies to the opposite side to counter-balance the movement. If we fell from the top, the injury might be serious. If we could be sure of only a broken leg, or even two of them, we might not make any effort to prevent the bus from turning over. But an injured spine might result from such a fall, so we prefer to take a chance up the line. The chances of being wounded, as against being killed, are three or four to one in our favour. We have often reckoned that the proportion of killed to wounded is one to four.

The buses come to a halt at Tertry and we climb down. Each Company advances separately, and when we have gone a mile or two up the road to Villeveque, we split up into smaller sections. The platoons march at ten-minute intervals. We know that we are rapidly getting nearer to the line.

In the late afternoon we rest a while, and then move forward again. Ahead of us is a railway embankment, but we cannot see beyond it. On the embankment is a large signboard with the name Marteville on it. On our side of it there are many dug-outs. They are cut right into the embankment. But when we arrive there, we find that they are already occupied by the Engineers. So we sit down outside to await orders.

On a stone about four yards away from me is a boy twenty years old. There is one other man between us. We hear the sound of rifle fire and machine-guns plainly. The front line is less than a mile ahead of us. But we are very well protected by the railway embankment. It is several yards thick, and many yards above us.

An occasional bullet goes over us, and we hear the noise of a ricochet at times. We do not know why they are firing high, but think that these bullets are aimed at a cross-road behind us, in the hope of catching some transport. We have often done this kind of thing ourselves. There are times when one feels that one must fire at something. In another part of the line, we used to hang corned beef tins from the barbed wire, and blaze away at them. When they fell we would take it in turns to crawl over the top and hang them up again. It was a terrible thing not to have anything to do, so we amused ourselves in this way. Only once was I sniped at while passing the time in this foolhardy manner. It is not only schoolboys who will get into mischief when they find time hanging heavily on their hands. Inanition can play strange tricks with adults too.

Without any warning the boy of twenty falls off his stone. He slithers to the ground and crumples up. We heard the sound of the bullet which struck him in the head. It came from somewhere on the left. We took no notice of it as it sounded almost like a spent bullet.

We jump up to help him, and see that his face is covered with blood. We feel in his pocket for his supply of iodine and first-aid field dressing, and bandage him. Then we carry him back to the MO. There are several others waiting to be attended to, but most of them are walking cases. They just sit about outside the dug-out waiting for their turn to go in. We explain to the orderly that this case is urgent, and we carry him into the dug-out. We cannot do anything more, so we just leave him there and go back to our places. Later in the evening we hear that he has died.

This is our first casualty in the new sector. It is cruel luck to be killed a mile behind the Front and in such a safe position. If he had been six inches to the right or left, he would still be with us. That is what the soldier calls luck. His name must have been on the outside of the bullet which killed him.

In a few days the postman will deliver a buff-coloured envelope to his parents in Worcestershire, to say that he has been killed in action. They will perhaps think of him as being foremost in the bayonet charge, or holding his trench against great odds. *Requiescat in pace.*

It is an unheroic way in which to die. But he died humbly as he had lived humbly. In other days he had milked cows and picked ripe plums and cherries in their season. He had often told me of the country lanes and the overhanging fruit in the paths through the Vale of Evesham, and I had promised to look him up and stay a night or two with him in the humble home he loved so well, if we both managed to survive the war.

He spoke with a peculiar drawl. One front tooth projected forwards and a wisp of hair would not be brushed backwards. To live with horses, and always near to the earth, was all that he asked in life.

We spend the night out-of-doors, and when morning breaks we go forward to relieve the Lancashire Fusiliers of the 32nd Division. A shallow communication trench connects with the front line. It is only chest-high, and is knocked in every few yards. The country on both sides is fairly open. There is no cover except the long grass. This stands two feet high in places.

Just ahead of me, I see a youth walking unsteadily. As he gets nearer, I note that he is an extraordinary colour. It is not ordinary paleness such as comes with loss of sleep and living out of the sun. He is more the colour of a sea-sick person – half yellow and half green. He sways from side to side in the narrow trench as though he were drunk, but he still carries his rifle with his arm through the sling.

As we come abreast, I see that he is wounded. He appears far too young for this kind of thing. On his chin the hair is still soft; he has hardly had his first shave. Behind his left ear, and a little lower, there is a ghastly gaping wound. A jagged piece of shrapnel has caught him. It has not been bandaged. You could put your clenched fist into it. It is terrible to look upon. He staggers and we support him. I light a cigarette for him and put it in his mouth. Then he collects his senses and goes on a few more paces. On his face there is a look of absolute terror. He is frightened, terribly frightened. He looks afraid, terribly afraid, of something that may be imminent. We have seen this kind of thing before. It bodes ill for him. He will need assistance to reach the dressing station.

We cannot stay to bandage him, as a relief is in progress. He moves down the section as we move up. We do not think he will get much further.

We hurry forward to get into position, as we should be heavily straffed if we were seen. There are always very sharp eyes to direct the fire of the artillery upon troops concentrated in the trenches. In a few yards we catch up with the remainder of our Company. They cannot move quickly, and frequently have to squeeze into the side of the communication trench to allow others to pass. A stretcher case comes along and we flatten ourselves out to give it room. The stretcher takes up practically the width of the trench. We cannot see the man upon it, as his head has been covered over. But we see that a leg has been shattered and his trousers and the canvas of the stretcher are soaked in blood. The bottom of the trench shows where the blood has dripped through.

There is no way to the rear other than by this trench. It would not be possible to go over the top, as one would be in full view of the enemy. Even stretcher-bearers would be fired upon immediately.

We keep low as we near the end of the trench. Then we run twenty yards across the open, and get into position along a sunken road. In peace time it had been a farm road through some fields. Immediately, we take off our entrenching tools, and begin to dig into the bank. The ground is hard and clayey. Only a small chunk comes out at a time. It takes three or four blows to dig out a piece, and we cannot use the spade end of the tool. We can only manage an inch at a time, and at the end of an hour we have not made much impression upon the bank in front of us. We dig feverishly and sweat like pigs. Our object is to make holes big enough to crawl into. We should then be safe from the sideways blast of shells. Only a howitzer could hurt us by scoring a direct hit upon us.

At the end of three hours we can dig no more. The deeper we go, the harder the ground becomes. It is almost like trying to chip off pieces of flint. The best of us have only dug a hole deep enough to squeeze a hip into. We are physically played out.

We do not know exactly how far the enemy is in front of us, but the distance cannot be great. He is well supplied with machine-guns, and the noise they make is very clear. They cannot be more than four hundred yards away. Isolated rifle shots warn us that the snipers are particularly busy. They are having a field-day. Our ears have become so accustomed to the sounds that we can even distinguish our own and the enemy's snipers.

Farther down the road, the stretcher-bearers run to a man who has been hit. He was also half-in and half-out of a funk-hole. This means that enfilade fire is being brought to bear upon us. The enemy is shooting down the road. This bodes ill for us.

Then follows a long burst of machine-gun fire. We recognise it as a Lewis gun. The enfilade fire ceases. Our men must have caught the sniper, and either killed him or compelled him to take cover.

The minutes drag by. We cannot quite understand the reason why we are in this road. We have not been told to do anything. We are just targets, even though unseen. The enemy evidently knows we are here, and intends to dislodge us. The minutes tick past slowly – we are just waiting. We cannot go back, and we have not been told to go forward. But even if the order came to advance, we could not do so. Ahead of us is a considerable slope, and we should simply be mown down by the machine-guns.

As we lie and press ourselves close to the earth, the bullets zip past us. But they are innocuous. We hear them all, but know that they can do us no harm, and do not mind them in the least. All we have to do is keep down. It is like hiding behind a four-foot wall with hailstones being blown by the wind slantwise over it. If we showed ourselves above the bank, we should fall back riddled with bullets. We just cling to our positions, and have to accept whatever the gods may send us. There is no possibility of being relieved, as we have only been under fire for a few hours, and in any case there are only a few casualties. Two days will pass before we shall go back again, and anything might happen in the meantime. So we just hang on like grim death. There is nothing that we can do to improve our lot, so we just lie doggo and hope for the best as the day drags along.

About three o'clock in the afternoon the machine-gun ceases. We breathe freely for half an hour, and think that the enemy has retired. But we are soon undeceived. They have found that we cannot be compelled to retire except by shell-fire. Perhaps they have brought up a battery of field-guns to dislodge us.

The first shell goes harmlessly overhead and we see it burst fifty yards behind us. It must have just skimmed over the road. Almost before we heard it coming, it exploded. We know it for a whizz-bang. They are murderous little devils as they come upon you without the slightest warning. The sound of the shell being fired, the noise of the explosion, and the sight of flying earth are all practically simultaneous, even if the shell drops far behind you. The French 75's are like that. So are our own 18-pounders.

The first shell is a range-finder. We have often experienced this kind of thing, and we know that the sunken road will be almost untenable in a few minutes. It is merely a question of time before a shell gets us. Three shells in a row is the rule; one beyond, one short, and the third in the middle is what we expect. We are impotent as we lie in the sunken road. There is nothing that we can do.

The second falls fifty yards short. It sends up a cloud of smoke, and the pieces of shrapnel go whining through the air. Several come in our direction, but do not quite reach us, and do no harm.

The third follows quickly upon the second, and then the whole battery opens up on us. We cannot move to the left or right. Every two yards there is a man, and as far as we can see between one explosion and the next, nobody else is any better off than we are in our position.

The shells crash down upon us. The earth round about us becomes convulsed. Some fall a little short and some go beyond us, but most of the shells burst above the road. The shrapnel spreads fan-wise. A sickening thud beside me makes me glance up. A piece of metal with rough edges, the size of a tea cup has buried itself in the bank. I touch it, and pull my hand away quickly. It is is almost white-hot. A few more inches would have been enough, and perhaps more than enough.

We are entirely helpless, and are pinned to the ground. They have got the range perfectly. I push my head as far as possible into the hole I have made, and put my stomach down to the ground. We all roll ourselves up like millipedes, and try to halve our bulk. Each time a shell comes close to us we press down upon ourselves. Our luck cannot possibly hold in this position. The world is, for us, full of strange noises and savage barks, and the cries of wounded men.

In the next funk-hole to mine is Polly, the platoon sergeant. He is not even two paces away from me. He wears the Mons ribbon, and has been out since 1914. He is the finest type of regular soldier I have ever known. It is a marvel that he keeps so calm. I throw him my cigarette half-finished. It is not often that he smokes, but he has asked me for a draw. I have never seen him angry or drunk. Very rarely, he has been a little befuddled. We all love him, and pull his leg about the time he dodged the trench-mortars. He was in the Mons retreat, then at Loos, Ypres, Givenchy, Festubert, La Bassée, Arras, High Wood, and other places where the fighting was fiercest. High Wood and Contalmaison were the worst of all, he has told us. The Battalion lost heavily there, and Polly was among the badly wounded.

He very seldom swears, but he turns to me and says we shall be damned lucky to come out of this action alive. He has scarcely finished saying it when he is fatally wounded. There is a blinding flash and a roar. Immediately behind us a shell hits the bank. It bursts backwards, and Polly seems to get it all to himself.

I go to him immediately, and do not mind the shelling. It goes on as fiercely as before. But I pay no attention to it, because of something to do. I pull down his trousers and rip out his shirt, and see that he is wounded in eight places. Five of them are in the legs. They might not be frightfully serious. None of us would mind them. But the three stomach wounds are terribly dangerous.

At a glance I see that little can be done for him. One wound is almost as big as a saucer, and the intestines hang out of it. He lies flat on his back, and the life goes out of his eyes. I pull out my iodine and bandages and try to help him. The lesser wounds bleed profusely, but I concentrate upon the large one. I push back the intestines, and stuff a whole bandage soaked in iodine into the wound. He tries to say something but cannot do so. I cannot make out a single word. His voice fades with each incoherent sound. He looks imploringly. He groans terribly, and I know that the end will soon come.

A volunteer climbs over the bank, and goes back for aid. I do not think he will get through the shell-fire; it looks like a curtain descending upon us. But in twenty minutes I see the MO coming on horseback. He gallops as hard as possible, but he does not reach us. Before he gets to the road he is hit by a shell. It is a direct hit, and horse and rider just disappear. One moment he is there; the next, he is not. He had only joined us a few days previously. His predecessor was also killed by shell-fire in the front line.

We cannot stand this punishment any longer, and we send up the SOS signal. In a minute our Divisional Artillery reply, and the eighteen-pounders begin their rapid fire. The SOS is the signal for drum-fire. We are glad Jerry is having hell knocked out of him.

Within a few minutes the shells all seem to be going one way. We breathe again, and thank heaven for the Artillery. The 4.5 howitzers join in, and we know that what we have received is no more than is being paid back. It gives us a little consolation.

Nine killed and sixteen wounded is the number of casualties in the platoon. Three of the wounded will easily get to England; they will not be out of hospital within six months. The others are not so serious. They will only go to the Base, unless there are crowds of wounded going down the line.

Polly is dead. We do not bury him, because he will be carried back over the top when night comes. We keep him beside us for the remainder of the day, and cover his face with his tunic. We put it over him because we cannot bear to look at him all the time; but sometimes we feel we want to see his face just once more while daylight lasts. We remove the tunic a little to one side, and then come away again. It is not curiosity on our part; it is a sign of affection, and we know that in a few more hours the opportunity will pass for ever. We shall not see the like of him again. He took me under his wing when I first came to the Company, and initiated me into the best ways of survival at the Front. He was a gentle soul and the greatest loss we have so far sustained. If there were more men like Polly in the Army, life would go along more smoothly and comfortably for everyone. He had not a single enemy, and we who knew him well held him in the highest regard. His patience was inexhaustible with the most backward among us.

He was always accessible, and spoke in a quiet manner to everybody. There was a very pleasant burr in the way in which he spoke, which reminded me of the yeomen of the west of England who live close to the soil. Perhaps he had been born and brought up in the countryside and learnt the manners and ways of the people who dwell there.

CHAPTER NINE

Over The Top: The Living and the Dead

The night passes quietly; neither side fires a shot, but the fireworks begin in front of us. We are glad that the Very lights go up, as we know that the enemy will not attack us. He merely wishes to know that we have not left our positions in the sunken road.

In the early morning a runner arrives from Headquarters. We are warned to be ready to attack at 7.30. An intense shrapnel barrage will be put down for ten minutes. Then we must go forward, and gain the crest of the slope. Not much opposition is anticipated as it is believed the enemy has retired his main forces. But we know that Jerry always leaves machine-gunners behind to inflict heavy casualties as he goes back.

By 6.30 it is daylight. We space ourselves out. One man to four yards is our strength. We make sure that our magazines are full, and that our bayonets are fixed securely to our rifles. By 7 a.m. all is ready for the attack. The signal will be a long blast on a whistle. It is not a big attack. Two Companies only will take part. We have been told our objectives, and cannot in any case make a mistake.

Our officer looks hard at his watch. As the time draws nearer, he becomes apprehensive, and every few seconds glances down.

We all feel the nervous strain, and wish we had not so long to wait. Each minute seems like ten. We wish that we were out of the trench and going forward. The worst part of an attack is immediately before the attack takes place. You can do nothing but sit or stand or crouch, and think. One's brain races, but time seems to stand still.

The minutes pass. Then the barrage begins. It shrieks overhead, and comes down on the ridge in front of us. We peep out over the top and get the lie of the land. There is not much wire ahead – only loose coils. The shells have time fuses, and most of them burst in the air. The shrapnel from them scatters in all directions. We see the puffs of grey-blue smoke, and hear the explosions and the whining of the fragments, as they hurry earthwards in search of victims. This morning the Germans are on the receiving end. We hope that they are having hell knocked out of them.

When the whistle is blown, some of us scarcely hear it. But we see some of our men climbing out over the grassy bank, and follow their example. We go forward at a steady trot, so as not to wind ourselves. Just to the left, a machine-gun fires. But the gunners are firing high, and the bullets go over our heads. When we are half-way up the slope the shell-fire increases, to give us extra protection.

We gain the top of the slope without a single casualty in our platoon, and jump down into the enemy's trench. A team of gunners hold up their hands. Near to them is their gun. A shell has just put it out of action, and beside it lie three men. The others are white-faced and wild-looking. We beckon to them to go the rear, and see them safely on the way. They go without an escort, as we cannot spare a single man. Before they have gone far, they will come upon our support line, and someone will be provided to take them back.

We set about making the trench more defensible, in case we are counter-attacked. The whole length of the trench, this work goes on. Except for an occasional shell, we are undisturbed, and the day passes quietly.

We take turns in doing sentry-go. Our method of choosing is to put the names into a hat, and the new sergeant draws them out two at a time. The first to be drawn take the first two hours' watch, and so on. I draw from four to six in the morning, and settle down in the open trench for the night.

It is moonlight, and before any of us can get to sleep, the Company runner arrives from Battalion Headquarters. He inquires for the officer in charge, and hands him a slip of paper. The old hands know the full significance of this act, and say that in the morning we shall go over the top again. They are able to smell trouble ahead. Their judgement is unerring.

In a short time we know that we are for it. A big attack has been planned to begin at 6.30 in the morning.

At four o'clock I go on sentry. The moon has long since disappeared, and the early morning is pitch-dark. There is nothing to be seen; one can only listen for any unusual sound. It is not our practice to use flares. We just lie doggo, with our rifles resting on the sandbagged parapet.

My mate stoops and lights a cigarette. It has probably supplied him with three smokes already. When the supply is running short, four pulls is the common practice. The last is always a long one, and the smoke is emitted a little at a time.

When Bill has finished his cigarette, he asks me to keep a good look-out, because he wants to relieve himself. There are not always conveniences at the Front, and one just disappears anywhere. He glides away in front of me. There is no sound of any kind, and I close my eyes. It is difficult to remain awake, and when there appears to be no need to be vigilant, one involuntarily relaxes. I do not fall asleep, but my mind is certainly not concerned with keeping guard.

Suddenly I hear someone shouting, but do not at first quite understand what it is all about. But in a moment or two I am wide awake, and have my rifle ready and pointing towards the enemy. I grip it tightly. Then I hear someone calling out, 'Cover him! Cover him! Cover him!' I recognise Bill's voice, and I stare hard into the blackness but can neither see anybody nor hear any footsteps. Two or three minutes pass. I can bear the suspense no longer, and call out to Bill. He replies that there is a Jerry coming in my direction.

Then I hear a voice which is clearly not an English voice. It calls 'Kamerad – pistolet! Kamerad pistolet!' I lie still, and hardly dare to breathe. My heart thumps as though it will burst. Then I hear the swish-swish of the moving grass, and a tall figure looms up in front of me. There is just sufficient light to see him at six yards' distance. When he sees me, he halts. He keeps calling out 'Kamerad – pistolet – pistolet!' I see that his right arm is held high above his head. With the left arm he points to the ground. He is very emphatic, and is clearly doing his utmost to make himself intelligible. If I were to shot him the bullet would go clean through him and through Bill too, so I do not fire.

He comes right up to where I am lying, and continues to shout the same two words. I cover him all the time with my rifle, and my bayonet. He looks away from them. The cold steel gleams in the very early morning. I get up, and do not take my eye off him. He is a big strapping fellow, and on his head is the familiar little round cloth cap. He is unarmed, and I know that he wishes to say that he has given himself up, and thrown away his rifle or revolver.

My mate comes in. When he speaks, the prisoner gets the fright of his life. He sees one man in front of him, and suddenly hears the voice of another behind him. Of the two, I do not know which is the more frightened. Both of them shake like aspen leaves, and the situation is not without its humorous side.

I had no wish to take a prisoner. He just gave himself up to me and I could not refuse to take him. If Bill had not been directly behind him, perhaps I should not have done so. He was just plain lucky. Thus does life at the Front sometimes depend upon purely fortuitous circumstances. I give each of the other two a cigarette, and we all three sit down and smoke in the early morning.

We line up in the trench, and a few minutes after six o'clock we are ready for the next attack. Our rifles rest against the front of the trench, and in places the tips of the bayonets project over the top.

When three loud blasts are blown on the whistle, we scramble up the side of the trench. Our rifles are pushed over the top. Above the screaming of the shells, we hear the murderous machine-guns as they traverse our line. The bullets search all round us. On my left, two men go down. One is hit in the forehead, and falls back into the trench. Subconsciously, we hear a thud as he strikes the ground.

Jones is more fortunate. He could scarcely have hoped for anything better. He is caught in the left knee, and in the fleshy part of the right leg. He just says 'Damn it!' and sits on the ground. He does not mean to curse his luck; it is just force of habit, when anything unexpected happens.

We cannot stay to help him, but note that he pulls his trousers down and unwinds his puttees. His hands are free and he can apply his own bandages. He will soon be found by the troops who are in support, and they will carry him back to the dressing-station. In a day or two, he may even find himself back in his native Lancashire, and hear the familiar sound of the clogs as they rattle down the street.

According to the plan of attack, we move forward very slowly. Our pace is almost that of a funeral procession. We carry our rifles with the left arm through the sling and the bayonets pointing upwards. Most of our shells burst two hundred yards ahead of us, and we know that the enemy position is thereabouts. If we hurried our pace, we should walk into our own shell-fire. We have five minutes to go across the open, and then the range will be lengthened and a curtain of fire will descend upon the second enemy position.

One of the guns continues to fire short. It is somewhere to the right of us. I hear a scream and see that Lance-Sergeant Hunt has fallen. A shell burst just behind him. Both his legs have been severed at the thighs. I spare him a moment, but see at a glance that I cannot do anything. It would need a skilled surgeon to help him. The arteries have been cut right through, and the blood spurts out with each beat of the heart. The ground around him is soaked. In a very few minutes he will be dead.

As I bend over him, he looks up and recognises me. I can see the life departing from him. He half smiles, and is just able to say, 'Give 'em hell.' I nod in reply.

I catch up with the others, and we carry our rifles with both hands, and double the last twenty yards to the enemy's trench. We jump into it. It is unoccupied.

We climb out of it again and go forward, seeking the protection of our own shells. Before we have gone fifty yards, we come under heavy rifle-fire. Then we see Jerry standing up in the long grass. Ahead of us there are thirty or more of the enemy. My platoon engages them, and we fire shot for shot. The distance between us lessens, and at twenty yards we can all see one another clearly. The grass is only half our height.

It is like shooting rabbits. At such a distance it should be impossible to miss one's target. We fire at least ten rounds each, but we have only six casualties. Two of them are wounded; four of them are killed outright. We get fifteen of the enemy. Perhaps they have not been trained as we have to get off fifteen rounds a minute.

Then we hear a sharp command. We do not know who utters it, except that it is an enemy officer or NCO. Immediately, the Germans throw down their weapons, put their arms above their heads, and walk towards us. We cease fire and prepare to take them prisoners. But before they have advanced six paces, the staccato voice again barks out. Instantly they drop into the grass and are lost to sight.

Then a machine-gun comes into play. It is trained upon us, and the bullets whiz past, terribly close. We fall to the ground because it is the only thing to do, and crawl away to lose ourselves in the grass. We go as cautiously as possible, so as not to give ourselves away. If the grass waved too much, they would rake us. In a minute or two, the fire ceases because they cannot see where we are, and do not waste their ammunition. We feel that we have done quite well. There are fifteen dead Germans for the loss of our lance-sergeant and four men in the attack.

A few of us come upon a German post. It is a small trench, only twenty yards long and four feet deep. It is well hidden by the grass and is L-shaped. Leading from it are several small dug-outs, each large enough for two or three men. Each dug-out has only a foot of earth for a roof, but we are safe from shrapnel and rifle-fire. We know that we cannot advance any further, because all the ground in front of us is under machine-gun fire. When we drop into the enemy trench we feel that we have been cut off. We have lost touch with the troops on our right and on our left, and we do not know whether they are in front of us or behind us. Our own advance was according to the time-table.

There are ten of us. Only shell-fire can dislodge us. Two of us keep a look-out. The others retire out of sight into the cubby-holes. We remain in this position all the morning. The Front has become quiet again. At intervals we hear bursts of machine-gun fire. Then they die down again. Sometimes a rifle cracks, and we know that the snipers are keeping a sharp eye open. Perhaps somebody away in the rear has moved and attracted attention.

At half-past one, the stillness is broken on our right. We cannot tell the distance, but it must be at least four hundred yards alway. We listen carefully and are able to locate the position. There is some shouting and a good deal of rifle and machine-gun fire. We guess that an attempt is being made to force the enemy to retire, but we cannot be sure of anything. The long grass completely hides our view.

The noise continues for a quarter of an hour, and we decide to try and find out the reason for it. Two of us go, and if we do not return, others will follow later. It is necessary that we should know what is happening, as the attack has been held up for several hours. Perhaps other troops have been thrown into the line. No message has reached us.

Nip follows me out of the trench. In action, he will not be separated from me. It is pathetic to see him hanging on. He is my senior by ten or fifteen years, but he seems to believe that his fate and mine hang together. I do not know whether it is fear for himself or for me that makes him stick to me. He makes me think of the little poem I learnt by heart as a child, and of the lines, 'I have a little shadow which runs in and out with me'.

To-day he looks more than usually pinched and half-starved. His one great fear is that he may get a stomach wound, and he continually impresses upon me the necessity for protecting the stomach when in action. Some months ago, he even wrote home for a body protector, and wore it for some time, until the others laughed him out of it. They called him 'The lady in corsets'. Perhaps it was because of the ridicule; or maybe it was the extreme discomfort of the shield which caused him to forget to bring it back when we were relieved.

We go at a snail's pace through the grass. A gentle breeze blows over it, and it waves like an English hay-field in a zephyr. As I crawl along, *ventre à terre,* I am reminded of a day long past when I searched for the nest of a skylark in a similar place. It took me an hour to find it. There were three lovely greenish-brown eggs in the nest. I recall that I had heard the lark singing high up in the sky, and it then swooped unerringly to its nest.

When we have gone a hundred yards, we find that the grass becomes shorter, and affords but little cover. We move in the direction from which the firing comes, but we are observed, and come under rifle-fire. In front of us is a shell-hole, and we run for it as being the only place of safety. We tumble into it, and consider ourselves fortunate to have found it. But it has other occupants.

In the shell-hole are two German soldiers. They are both dead, and we think that they have been caught in the barrage before the attack began. They do not appear to have been badly knocked about. They just lie as though they are sleeping, except that their eyes are wide open. They cannot do us any harm, and we decide that it would serve no useful purpose to pitch them out of the shell-hole. So we all four share the same quarters – two alive and two dead. They make strange bed-fellows, but we pay no attention to them.

When the firing dies down, Nip suggests that we should eat our dinner. The sun has passed its zenith, and a cool wind has sprung up. We take off our haversacks, and ransack them for our rations. We feel that we could do justice to an eight-course dinner. Life in the open makes us terribly hungry, but we do not find much to appease our hunger.

I produce half a loaf of bread and a tin of beef, and Nip provides the other half of our dinner. He always has something up his sleeve, and pulls out a tin of pork and beans. This is a real delicacy and does not often come our way. A tin between us is a most unexpected windfall. One tin to six men is the rule in our Company, and we have only been having pork and beans once a week.

As we spread out our food upon our haversacks, we realise that we might have been much worse off than we find ourselves. The bread and the beef are good. The pork and beans would be much better if we could heat the tin in hot water. That is our usual method of preparing them. But a fire is out of the question. So we both dip our spoons into the common tin, and even the most unattractive lumps of fat are eaten with avidity. We wash the food down with cold tea. As far as possible, Nip has provided for every contingency. He seems to be gifted with second-sight at times. His hard upbringing may have been responsible for it. He had often gone short of almost everything when he was young, and never in his life had there been a surplus of anything.

After we have finished eating, we each decide to smoke a cigarette. 'Red Hussars' is our favourite brand. We lie back on the slope of the shell-hole, and watch the smoke go curling up in the air. We blow rings to pass the time. I have never succeeded in blowing a good ring. Nip seems to put half of his cigarette into his mouth; it becomes soaked, and he pinches off a bit from time to time. The fact of the matter is that he is not really a smoker. He wastes the greater part of each cigarette.

As the afternoon advances, we decide to sleep. We do not know anything, except that we are in a shell-hole with two dead men, and that the general attack has not succeeded. The machine-gun fire was too much for us. There are limits to the punishment one can take.

A little shelling goes on, but it does not trouble us. Both sides fire to the rear. We can do no good by remaining awake, and we cannot possibly leave the shell-hole until night comes to cover our movements. If an attack were to develop, we should be awakened.

We are tired out, and feel the need of sleep. The afternoon has become chilly, and we decide to make use of the two German overcoats. They do not serve any purpose in keeping the corpses warm. We turn the Jerries over and remove their overcoats. Then Nip and I lie down, and spread both coats over us. It is like having two blankets.

We fall asleep and are untroubled by anything. But even in the shell-hole they do not allow us to rest for long. In the Army, it is a rule never to leave a person undisturbed. In less than half-an-hour we are awakened by the roar of an aeroplane engine. This does not worry us as we recognise the sound as one made by our own planes. In a minute or two we locate it, and as it comes nearer, we see the circles of red, white and blue painted under its wings. Our feeling is one of elation because this gives us confidence. It is the first sight of our own people we have had for hours. We believe that there are still people who are taking a friendly interest in us.

We turn over, and try to go to sleep again. But in a few minutes the plane returns, and flies above us at half its former height. At the Front this is almost an every-day sight, and we think the observer is spotting, to try to find out the positions of the hostile troops. If he succeeds in locating them, our artillery will be given the signal, and the machine-gun nests will be destroyed.

The aeroplane thunders past over our heads, and a magazineful of bullets is fired at us. We do not understand the reason for this act, as the circles clearly show it to be one of our own machines. Then we suspect that the enemy have captured it and are using it against us. It might cause hundreds of casualties before being brought down. All round us the earth is spattered with bullets.

When the aeroplane has gone a short distance, it swoops down like a hawk falling upon its prey. Then it turns and comes straight at us again. Each time it flies at half its previous altitude. It comes towards us like a mad thing. It cannot be satisfied. We cower. But our bodies have a certain size beyond which we cannot reduce them, even though we make ourselves as small as possible. The engine seems to tear the skies, and as I glance upwards I see the Lewis gun directed at us. It just spits fire.

It is impossible to explain why we are not hit. It just happens. The bullets fall into our shell-hole, and even on that side of it on which we lie. They go 'plop' into the ground. Any one of them might give us six months in England, or cause us to be referred to as 'killed in action'. That is all our home folk would know about the inglorious end. The rest would be left to their imagination.

Doubtless, the awkward angle, and the speed at which the machine travels, make the firing difficult. Twice they have fired at us. The plane spins round for a third attempt. In a flash it occurs to me that the pilot and the observer think that we are German soldiers because they see the field-grey coats which cover us. In a second, I pull them off and throw them away. Our khaki uniforms may save our lives.

The plane swoops still lower, and rushes at us like a terrified devil at tree-top height. But no shots are fired. The man behind the gun leans out over the side of the aeroplane. We see his head quite clearly, but the rest of his body is under cover. He has already recognised us as Tommies, and sized up the situation. He waves his hand as the machine flashes past us. It gathers momentum and is soon lost to sight.

Nip and I are like two scalded cats. We have had the life frightened out of us. We lie in the shell-hole, shake like jelly-fish, and stream with perspiration. We have had what the soldier calls 'the fear of death' put into us. We light our cigarettes to steady ourselves as we lie flat out upon the ground. Neither of us is able to speak for several minutes. It has been a nerve-shattering experience, and we do not feel like talking.

As the afternoon passes and the evening draws on, we become convinced of the necessity for re-joining our platoon. We can do nothing in our present position. We have not even found out any useful information, and when the light fails sufficiently, we venture out of the shell-hole and crawl back in the direction from which we have come. At first we make no sound whatever. Then, when we think that we cannot be far from our starting point, we call softly.

We have been given up for lost, and the others are surprised to see us come in. They had been speculating on our chances, and decided that the snipers had spotted us, and blotted us out.

At night, we receive orders to retire. The casualties in our Battalion have been heavy, and we assume that we shall be relieved and go back for a rest. But this luck does not come our way. We go back only to straighten out the line, and occupy the German trench which we captured in the morning.

CHAPTER TEN

No Prisoners Today!

An extra rum ration has come up for us. It is not often that we are treated so liberally. This is the second within eight hours. The first was to keep us warm during the night. There are no dug-outs, nor shelters of any kind, and we were glad of the issue. The benefit is almost instantaneous.

The tipplers amongst us swear that when the war is over, they will go and live in Jamaica. They cannot imagine anything better than to lie in the sun all day and to drink neat rum.

The second ration is supposed to give us Dutch courage. It might fulfil its purpose if it were handed out in more liberal doses. There is no doubt about its strength, but half-an-inch in a tin mug is scarcely enough to make us mad. It does not even make us merry. But everyone of us welcomes it.

In another half-hour we shall go forward again. This will be the third time 'over the top' within forty-eight hours. The artillery has been strengthened, and a large number of French 75's will help with the bombardment at Maissemy.

Behind us, the guns stand almost wheel to wheel, and the attack of yesterday will be repeated on the same scale. We expect to advance at least two miles.

Five minutes before we go over, a message is passed down the trench. 'No prisoners today.' We have not the men to spare to escort them back, as our Divisional losses have been heavy. The enemy's machine-gunners have done their work thoroughly, and perhaps this command is in the nature of a quid-pro-quo.

The barrage is a perfect one. We have never seen better. Not a shell falls short. They shriek over our heads, but we do not even duck. We fancy that we can tell the difference between the 75's and our own eighteen-pounders. The 75's are very much like the German whizz-bangs.

If they had given us a barrage like this before, we should not have been held up. Away on both sides of us we can see the bursts of the shells. There are hundreds of them every minute. We feel confidence in our gunners and in ourselves. We feel that everything will go well on this occasion.

Every square yard in front of us comes in for treatment. Hundreds of guns are being used, and Jerry can scarcely ever have had a greater pounding. The earth leaps skywards. We hear the roars of the bursting shells, see the whole of our part of the Front enveloped in smoke and flame, and smell the fumes as they are carried on the breeze in our direction.

Most of us look out over the parapet. We do not feel any sense of danger as Jerry is so completely paralysed by the shell fire. We know that he is lying as low as possible, and hugging the earth in his hope of escaping the bursting shells. We have often done the same thing. We feel pity for him, but it is not an unmixed pity, because we know that in the success of the bombardment lies our own hope of safety. His machine-guns would only mow us down again. We watch, fascinated, and wonder what awaits us in a few minutes.

We come under machine-gun fire again. The assault has been in the nature of a picnic up to this point. The shells have effectively screened us, and forced the Germans to keep their heads down.

When the range is increased, they creep out of their shell-holes, and man their trenches again. It is a miracle that any of them are still alive.

The rat-tat-tat breaks out once more, and we realise that the fight is just beginning. One gun appears to be trained upon us. The bullets sweep us, shoulder-high. We cannot see the Jerries. Our casualties begin. We keep on going forward. There is no question now of retiring. We do not even lie down. We just keep on moving, though at a quicker pace than before.

Four men in my section have gone down. I do not know whether they have been wounded or killed. Something hits my steel helmet and knocks it to one side and half-way down over my eyes. I just push it back again. There is no time to stop.

A few moments later we spot the machine-gun and the men who use it to fire at us. We run towards them, zig-zagging slightly. This makes it more difficult for them to aim at us. We do not go far to the left or right, as this would take time. We lower our rifles, and run at them. They are only fifty yards from us, but they continue to fire. We lose two more men, but the distance between us is rapidly lessening.

When we are only twenty yards away, they cease firing and throw up their hands. They stand in a shallow trench up to their knees. Two machine-guns are on the parapet, and strewn all round then are belts of ammunition. We know that these are the very belts that have been used against us, and that our luck has been in, or we should be lying beside our unfortunate comrades. From one machine-gun hangs a half-empty belt.

There are eight Jerries altogether, and five of us. We do not even consult together to decide what to do. It is understood perfectly what we shall do. We shall just give them a dose of the medicine which they have meted out to our comrades. We shall not spare a single one of these Boches. They stand before us, and seem to know that we have taken on the role of executioners. Two or three of them call out – *'Kamerad! Kamerad!'* They are defenceless, but they have chosen to make themselves so. We did not ask them to abandon their guns. They only did so when they saw that those of us who were not mown down were getting closer to them, and that the boot was now upon the other foot.

We do not waste any time, but pair off, like two rival sections at school. I take the left hand man. He can easily give me twenty years, and his age must be at least forty. But that does not avail him anything. He has not shaved for several days. On his head is the ludicrous little hat. It has a blue ribbon around it. A Prussian, I register mentally. Then I think that it is curious how the mind works even in action. He is a fine upstanding man, with the strength of an ox. But the strength of a Samson would avail little in such circumstances.

I raise my rifle to the shoulder. He is only eight yards from me. He does not move, but squeals like a kitten that has strayed from home. He fixes his bottle-green eyes upon me, and I see that he changes colour. He becomes ash-grey and in those eyes there is a look of hatred, defiance, fear and terror. Then, as a last resort, he calls *'Kamerad!'*

I press the trigger and fire. It is quite impossible to miss at such short range. He gives one piercing shriek, jumps clean off the ground, then crumples up. It is a reflex action.

His seven companions are treated in the same way. They lie beside their machine-guns. We survey our handiwork with satisfaction, and do not feel any sense of pity for the dead Jerries. We feel that we have begun the day well, and sit down for a moment to take stock of our surroundings and to think of our friends who have been wounded and killed by these machine-gunners.

In front of us are eight dead Jerries and two machine-guns. Clearly someone must stay to look after them. If we do not do so, the 'moppers-up' will lay claim to them. We have no desire to pass on the honour to somebody else. Our casualties have been heavy, and we really cannot spare anyone to remain behind. But one of us is well-liked and has had three years at the Front. He is a corporal and a good soldier. He has often done enough for glory, but no-one has ever rewarded him. Twice he has been recommended, but nothing has come of it.

Our morning's haul is a good one. Many a time a Victoria Cross has been given for far less than two machine-guns and eight corpses. This will mean a Distinguished Conduct Medal at least, and we reckon that he has often earned it. So we unanimously decide for him to sit tight, and to tell his own story when an officer comes his way. We tell him to deal only with a senior officer, and to insist on being present when taking the guns back to the rear. Otherwise, someone else may jump his claim.

He thinks that if he says that we were held-up by machine-gun fire, and that he rushed them single-handed, and shot the teams, the story will go down. We cannot think of anything better, and agree to back him up. Then we leave him in possession. He sits on a dead Jerry, pulls out a cigarette, and lights it. As we glance back, he looks as though the world belongs to him. He gives us a friendly wave of the hand.

Suddenly we see a German soldier dart out from near us. He is young – not more than twenty-five – and we recognise him as an officer. Probably he was the subaltern in command of the machine-guns. He runs hell-for-leather in front of us, and is soon two hundred yards away. He behaves just like a rabbit bolting from cover.

Green, our Number One on the Lewis gun, calls to me. He says he thinks the target is easily worth a magazine. The officer quickly gains ground, until he is three hundred yards away. Green rests the gun on my right shoulder, and blazes away at him. The first burst misses him, but before half the magazine has been fired, the Jerry goes down. It is a fine piece of work. It is worth twenty bullets to see him tumble over.

We run down the slope to where the German officer lies. He is a very good-looking fellow with a clear pink-and-white complexion, a finely-chiselled nose, and an agreeable mouth and chin. He faces upwards. His grey-blue eyes are still open. His head is clean cut through the top. It is as though one used an axe and gave two chops with it. There is a deep V-shaped wound in the skull. It runs the whole length of it. It must have killed him in an instant.

On his tunic is the ribbon of an Iron Cross, and we are glad that we have got him and his team of gunners. They have probably caused much destruction. Now they have run their course.

Our prize scrounger immediately begins to hunt around for souvenirs. He has not often had such a haul from one corpse. The Iron Cross ribbon only serves to whet his appetite. In a moment he cuts it off and puts it away safely. Then he goes through all the pockets. He comes across a revolver, many letters, some photographs, a good deal of money, and finally a wrist watch. He estimates the total value at three hundred francs. It is not often that he comes across such good fortune, and he smacks his lips with satisfaction.

The noise of our Lewis gun and the cheer we make as we run towards the officer, startle some other Jerries. They seem to come from nowhere as though the earth were sick of them and disgorged them. They converge as they run, and then disappear. We know what this means, and our next business is to try and discover their hiding place.

At first, we walk quickly to cover the ground. Then when we judge that we cannot be far from it, we search carefully for a dug-out. In a few minutes we come upon it. It is cleverly concealed, and from the air it could not be seen. All the earth has been moved to a distance, and there is nothing to indicate its presence.

We do not know whether it is a deep dug-out or a shallow one. But that does not worry us. We can very quickly find this out. What we do know is that it is probably the place into which the

Jerries have disappeared. So many men do not suddenly exist and then cease to exist.

We gave the enemy credit for more common sense and field-craft. In an attack, a dug-out is a suicidal hole. You cannot defend yourself, and the other man has you entirely at his mercy. Every one of us at the Front has had this impressed upon him times without number.

The purpose of a dug-out is to give shelter and protection during a bombardment, and when one is not actually on duty. But when the enemy advances, all troops are advised to leave their dug-outs to meet the attack. To remain underground is to court disaster.

Perhaps the Jerries saw no other chance of escape. In retiring, they would be observed by their own troops, and shot. Or they might run into our men away to the right or left of us. If we had not seen them, before they disappeared, it is possible that we should never have guessed that there was a dug-out in the vicinity. In this case, they would have been safe until we passed them by. Then they would emerge and attack us from behind, or they would stand an excellent chance of surrendering themselves. We do not want any prisoners today. We are not in the mood for encumbrances, and least of all for the human kind. Besides this, it is not often that we have the chance of such a good haul so cheaply.

In action, we do not trust the enemy. So we do not stand in front of the dug-out steps. If we were to do so, we should be outlined against the sky, and be easy targets for those down below. The novice might stand there and call upon them to surrender.

We stand back from the mouth of the dug-out, and shout out 'Jerry!' There is no reply. We call a second time. There is still no answer. We decide that we cannot all be mistaken but we never think of going down to see if it is occupied. Instead, one of us takes out a hand-grenade, and says that we shall soon know whether they are there or not.

He pulls out the pin, counts two, and bends over the top of the hole. Then he hurls the bomb down. In three seconds it explodes. They are vicious things, and we hear the roar of the bomb as it bursts. This is accompanied by the screaming of the enemy. They realise that they are caught, and we hear them talking. They are like rats in a trap and there is no escape possible. The best that they can hope for is captivity, and they cannot even be sure of that.

We stand back in line, with our rifles ready. In each magazine there are fifteen rounds. We call to Jerry to come up. The talking down below is followed by silence. Then we hear footsteps as the first one comes up the steps.

He emerges from the dug-out with his arms above his head and his back towards us. When he has walked forward twelve paces, one of us aims and fires. He just drops in his tracks.

The talking down below begins all over again. But we hold the whip hand, and we determine to get rid of the lot of them. We do not know how many there may be, but the number must be considerable, judging from the volume of sound that comes up.

A second one comes out of the opening. He does exactly as the first man did. When he sees his companion, he utters a scream, for he knows that the same fate awaits him.

We take it in turns to shoot. When the second shot is heard, they all know, without any doubt, that the end is near. Someone begins to whine, but we are merciless. For several days they have given us hell with their machine-guns and their field-guns. We have lost good men and good comrades.

It is not often that we are in a position to demand such ready retribution. We do not fail to take advantage of the situation. They would only eat good men's rations.

If the boot were on the other foot, we do not doubt what would happen. The position has often arisen, though this is our first experience of it. We are thankful that the situation is not reversed.

We hurry them on by throwing another bomb down the stairs. There is not the rest of the day to finish off the job. They come out, one by one. In less than half-an-hour the dug-out is cleared. Thirty-six Jerries lie piled up twelve yards from the entrance. There are probably others down below. We do not go down to see, but in order to avoid any possibility of error, we throw our remaining bombs down the steps.

The five of us feel that we have amply avenged Polly and those of our platoon who have gone west in the last few days.

It has been hot work and the nervous strain has been terrific. We sit down and light cigarettes, and view the pile in front of us. If we could often catch them like this, the war would soon be over.

The scrounger is irrepressible. Death, to him, means no more than life. While we rest, he goes in search of souvenirs. He turns over the corpses, and quickly goes through the pockets. He takes possession of anything that is likely to be of value. He fills his own haversack and even commandeers another. In a few minutes he comes back to us, and smiles as though he has found great treasure.

The advance is a walk-over. It seems that it will be endless. We go forward without very much opposition, and do not see many enemy soldiers. A long-range gun fires spasmodically, but we do not pay any attention to it. It does not aim especially at us, and even the shells which it fires do not all come in our direction.

We could easily dribble a football along. The ground is not much broken, and we could keep in line and pass the ball to one another. It is a one-sided game; there is only khaki to be seen, apart from a few field-grey corpses. These lie about in ones and twos, but nowhere are they numerous.

It is our belief that the enemy has retired to a stronger line of defence, 'according to plan'. This is the first time that we have seen the line so thinly held. Perhaps he pinned his faith on the skill and courage of his machine-gunners to hold us up again. They have often done so, and allowed the main body of his troops to get back in safety.

The country is undulating, and we swing along at an easy pace. There are but few obstructions. In a quarry, beside a main road, we come across a field kitchen. It has been in the hands of the enemy for many months, and on it is the name of our regiment. It was the property of another Battalion, and was abandoned when the enemy broke through the line and forced the Battalion to retreat in disorder. Perhaps the Germans have made use of it to cook for their own troops in the field. It has obviously been well looked after, and shines as though it has been made ready for a Divisional Show. Jerry is thorough in everything that he does. We admire him for his diligence and attention to details.

When we have advanced nearly three miles we are halted. To us, it appears that it would be possible to go farther as we seem to have Jerry on the run. But doubtless the authorities know what they are doing. At any moment the enemy resistance might stiffen, and a counter-attack would drive us back again and inflict serious losses. It is good to be wise in time. Perhaps at long last our leaders have come to realise that we are expendable.

In an attack you have always two things to consider; the enemy and yourself. Perhaps that is why we are halted. The transport and the guns have to move forward to keep pace with us. It is not wise to outdistance them, as we rely upon them for food and protection. In the evening they will come forward when the darkness will hide all their movements. Every available track will then become a highway.

We occupy high ground. It is level where we are, and also for some distance ahead of us. Beyond that, away to the front of us, it falls gently away.

We are really making for a large town. It lies to our left front, and is about twelve miles away. We are just able to see a part of it in the distance. In a week we shall reach it if our present rate of advance continues. Perhaps the Huns will destroy this town before we can get there. They have already destroyed so much in this fair land. There are man-made ruins over very large parts of it.

Some of us are hoping that we may have billets there. It seems an age since we were in a town or slept in a decent bed. Of late, we have done little else but attack the enemy. Our pay has accumulated, and we have not drawn a single franc for several weeks. We promise ourselves a good time when we move out of action again.

The order has reached us to dig-in where we find ourselves, and to hold on at all costs until we are relieved. We get in touch with those on either side of us, and thus form a line. It is a thin line, as many of our troops have fallen. It was not easy to overcome the enemy at all points.

Bill and I decide to dig-in together. It is better to have a partner while things are quiet than to be all on your own. We take off our entrenching tools and set about making a funk-hole for ourselves. It is not our intention to make a deep hole. The soldier never works unnecessarily, and we do not think that we shall be long in these positions.

There is no sound of gun-fire, and we might be a hundred miles away from any scene of war. If we can make a hole two feet deep to tuck ourselves into, we shall be satisfied. The afternoon is gloriously fine, and the sun shines down upon us. We work in a very leisurely manner, and in a couple of hours we make ourselves comfortable. We get into our hole and soon fall asleep. We do not awaken until all the warmth goes out of the sun.

On both sides of us we hear chattering. It is our own men. Apart from this, the evening is quiet. Some crickets chirp in the grass and the midges buzz all round us. The shadows lengthen and the night steals on. We do not know how far away we are from the enemy. No sounds reach us from in front, except the rumble of horse transport and the noise of motor lorries. They may be miles away, as the slightest disturbances carry a long distance in the stillness of the night.

But even these sounds tell us that there is an enemy ahead, and that he is not inactive. Perhaps at this very moment he may be concentrating troops from another part of the line where he is not being attacked.

But we live only in the present, and do not worry much about what may happen several days hence. We have very little control over the present, and none at all over the future.

Towards midnight, the ration party reaches us. We hear them crawling as they seek to find us. The line is not well defined, and they just move along until they meet someone. A corporal accompanies them to see that the food is delivered safely. They carry sand-bags, and in them are the rations for the whole of the Company. They consist of bread, biscuits, cheese, cigarettes, tinned beef and tea. Two ounces of tea per person is what we are allowed.

We prefer to have tea out of the dixie-can when possible, as two ounces per person per day does not go far. The tea is useless to us just now as we are unable to make a fire. But we put it away in our haversacks as though it were gold dust, and promise ourselves an extra brew when we can again light a fire to boil the water. In the meantime, chlorinated water will suffice to quench our thirst.

We think that a mistake has been made. The rations are more than usual. Then the corporal explains that each of us is really getting two shares as the Company has lost half of its men in the last three days. We had entirely overlooked this fact.

What pleases us most is the generous ration of rum. It is the most that we have ever had at a time. The corporal himself dishes it out. He uses a tin mug for the purpose. Each of us receives nearly half a mugful. Only the older hands are able to drink it in one gulp. It is just like fire-water and burns as it goes down.

Even before I have finished drinking my ration I know that I have had enough. But wisdom does not always come with knowledge. I gulp it down because the night is chilly, and the hours from twelve till six are long. At two o'clock it will be my turn to go on guard, so I determine to fortify myself, and chance the consequences.

In a few minutes my head swims and I become unsteady on my feet. I am fully conscious of my peculiar feelings. It is the first time that this has ever happened to me, but I know full well that I am rapidly becoming drunk.

Then I begin to laugh and become garrulous. I do not know what I talk about, or whether it is sense or nonsense. I only know that I talk and go on talking, like a patient coming out of chloroform.

Bill remonstrates with me and says that Jerry will hear the noise. I had entirely forgotten that such a person existed, and the name awakens in my mind an association of ideas. I remember that he is an enemy, and that I have been fighting him. Then I stand bolt upright, and challenge him loudly to come over and fight.

In the moonlight, it is a foolish thing to do. But when one is drunk one does not act rationally. A little reasoning is perhaps all that is possible, but the mind refuses to work in the same way as when one is sober.

I do not know if I am seen by the enemy or if he merely chances a shot at me. But in any case he hears me and in a very short time a machine-gun fires in my direction. The bullets whistle past me. Then Bill pulls hard at one of my ankles, and I fall into our funk-hole and in a minute or two am fast alseep. It is the very best thing that could possibly happen to us all, as I have become a real danger to the community.

I do not remember anything that happens during the night, and only wake up again just before six o'clock in the morning. The probability is that I should have slept for hours longer, had I not been forcibly awakened. My time on sentry has been taken by Bill; he has done four hours instead of two. I should have been useless in any case.

All around me the world seems to be coming to an end. The enemy's heavies drop shells all along our line. They are 5.9's, and burst with a deafening roar. Then comes the command, 'Stand to!' In a moment I awaken out of my lethargy, and no one could possibly guess that I had just come out of a drunken sleep. My faculties are wide awake, and in an instant I tumble to what is going on around me.

We lie flat-out upon the ground and our rifles point forward. An attack is expected at any moment, and we prepare to meet it. To save time, we undo the buttons of several of the pockets of our equipment, so that our ammunition may be taken out quickly. We even place several clips on the ground beside us in order that we may re-load as rapidly as possible when the magazines are empty. Fifteen rounds to the minute is what we have been trained to fire, and most of us can manage this without much difficulty. A good volume of fire often prevents an attack from developing, and we know from experience that rapid fire has a psychological effect even if it does not cause many casualties among oncoming troops.

The attack does not develop. Fritz merely gives us half-an-hour's punishment. Then all is quiet again, and we get the command 'Stand down!' By half-past six we resume our positions in our funk-holes.

Then we eat our breakfast. Bill and I agree upon a chunk of bread and a slab of cheese. Afterwards, we smoke, and then make up our minds to sleep.

Sleep is the biggest problem of all at the Front. It is even more important than the problem of food. There are so many occasions when it is impossible to obtain it, no matter how much it may be desired or become necessary. The only rule governing it is to sleep when you have the slightest opportunity to do so.

At mid-day we are treated to another dose of shell fire, and again we 'Stand to'. They crump all round us, but do not attack. In the evening the hymn is repeated. Each time, it is only the heavies that blast us. It is really retaliation for our having driven them out of their positions.

The field guns remain unusually quiet in order not to give away their positions. They cannot be far from us, but we do not see a single flash. Our aeroplanes have the complete mastery of the air. For every Jerry plane we see, there are a dozen of our own. They pass high over us, searching for the enemy's batteries, but they are unable to detect them. They have been well concealed with coverings of grass and branches. Fishing nets are a common device. The grass is woven through them, and leaves are then interlaced so that from the air the observers see only what appears to be ordinary bush.

When night comes, we are warned to be ready to move back out of action. We collect our few belongings and leave most of our ammunition in our funk-hole. It is heavy to carry back, and may prove to be of service to the relieving troops. But if they do not use it, it will be salvaged by those who are appointed to range over the battlefield. Not that this worries us in any case, as we shall be supplied with the usual hundred and twenty rounds when our turn comes again to move back into action.

Just after midnight, we hand over our line to a Battalion of Highlanders. To reach us, they crawl upon their hands and knees. We think that they are never coming, and begin to despair of ever going back again. Then we hear the rustle of the grass and the unmistakable sound of their voices, though they do not talk above a whisper.

Our last duty is to tell them all that we know concerning the enemy in front of us. This does not amount to much. We merely say that we do not know how far off Jerry is, as he has not given himself away. For this reason, we advise them to lie low and not to chance their luck at all.

Then we move back. Bill and I creep along until we think we can safely stand. The farther away we get from the enemy, the faster our pace increases. We do not know where we are going, although the assembly spot for the Battalion has been made clear. In the darkness we cannot see anything, so we resolve to walk for three hours, and to make inquiries when daylight comes. The remainder of the Battalion doubtless do the same thing.

We stumble along, and swear occasionally when we stub our toes against some unseen obstacle. Finally we come to rest, and sleep on the ground. All the plagues of Egypt would not awaken us.

At Maissemy the Germans have taken another hammering. They are not being allowed any respite. They were well entrenched along the high ridge, with much barbed wire in front of them. From their commanding positions they could see many miles ahead, as well as to the right and left. But we drove them out of these places and then over the ridge. As long as they could hang onto the high ground no advance by us would have been possible. Our losses have not been unduly heavy.

The Battle of Marteville and the Battle of Maissemy were two battles of the Hindenburg Line toward which the Germans were fighting a stubborn and skilful rearguard action.

CHAPTER ELEVEN

We Go in With the Tanks

The enemy has vacated his line and we move up to take over new positions somewhere in the region of Fresnoy-le-Petit. Ahead of us is a large wood. It is at least a mile long and nearly half a mile in depth. We have been given the task of clearing it. It has not been the least bit knocked about, because it was well behind our line at one period of the war, and later, when the Germans advanced, it was many miles to the rear of their trenches.

It is not known if the enemy is in strength there or not. We do not even know if it is occupied. But we are afraid of it because it looks dark and foreboding. The cover would be excellent, and the ground slopes away both to the right and left of the wood, affording good observation for miles around.

We form up four hundred yards in front of the wood, and advance to clear it. We are widely spread-out, both because the Battalion is not numerically up to strength, and also to afford little fodder for the enemy's cannon. Our attack is really in the nature of an experiment. It is to attract the enemy's fire if he is entrenched in the wood. If the attack is repulsed, a big attack will be made later to clear the Germans out.

A few rifle shots are fired at us, but we do not have any

casualties until we are within a hundred yards of the wood. The German snipers are not what they once were, and the shots appear to be fairly wide of us. Then a machine-gun fires. But even this does not seem to fire as maliciously or with such effect as in other actions. Only three of my platoon fall, and of the three only one is killed outright.

We advance in short rushes as we have been trained to do. Ten yards at a time is about the limit. Then we fall to earth and catch our breath. In a minute we rush again, then we once more get down. The last twenty yards are done at a stretch, and we jump into the undergrowth on the edge of the wood.

Before we have gone ten yards into the wood, we spot a machine-gun. Beside it there are three gunners. They are standing, and appear not to wish to fire at us. From behind the tree-trunks we shout to them. They put up their hands, and we know from the fact that nobody fires upon them, that they are an isolated team who have been sacrificed. They have been left behind to hold up our attack, while the main body of the enemy have retired.

They decide that the part which they can play will make no considerable difference to winning the war, and by surrendering, they can possibly save their lives. If they showed any fight we should certainly kill them.

We go forward, moving cautiously all the time, and take them prisoners. They are only youths, and cannot have had much training. Perhaps this is the first time they have been in the line. We beckon to them to pick up their gun, and then put one man in charge of them. He will see them to the edge of the wood, and there pass them over to the troops who are in support. Then he will return to us again.

The little opposition we encounter encourages us, and we become much more venturesome. The light inside the wood is not bright. Overhead, we see the blue sky only in patches; it is broken by the tree-tops. There are oaks and pines and plane trees and beeches, and deep-green, holly bushes. Overhead, a squirrel runs along a branch of a tree, and leaps from one tree to another as though it resents being disturbed in its lovely surroundings. If it could speak, it would say that men have no right to bring war into its haunts.

Soon after we have got under cover, an aeroplane passes overhead. We know from the noise of its engine that it is an enemy plane. It is joined by a second and then by a third aeroplane. All three of them pass over the wood, then hover like hawks waiting to attack. We hear a swish. It becomes louder and louder, and then the wood is torn with agony. As a valley holds the sound of a crack of thunder on the mountains round about, the wood reverberates with the noise of the exploding bombs. Chunks of iron are flung in all directions, and huge branches of trees creak and groan and drop heavily to earth. Big trees are blasted out by the roots, and in falling knock down other trees which are near them.

We cower under the pine logs, and do not know if the airmen are bombing us in particular, or merely trying to kill English soldiers. Our attack upon the wood has been observed, and the place has rapidly become a death-trap from which there is no escape. We know now why we were allowed such an easy entry into the wood.

Though we are really fairly safe under the pine logs, the ghastly noise of the exploding bombs, and the crashing of the trees to earth, are sufficient to make cowards of us all. Only a direct hit from a bomb could really do us much harm, though the danger of shell-shock is always present. But none drop upon us; the nearest is fifty yards away. The fragments come whizzing through the air towards us, and fall harmlessly into the soft ground. Some pieces fall short, and the others go over us. A few hit the logs and embed themselves in them.

Our Archies blaze away at the aeroplanes, and between the

tree-tops we see the balls of smoke as the shells explode. We have never seen an aeroplane hit by an anti-aircraft gun. Perhaps the value of anti-aircraft lies in frightening the airmen and driving them away from their target.

When they have dropped their load of bombs, the aeroplanes rise higher and go back over their own lines. We look out to see the damage that has been done.

The wood looks as though a hurricane has passed by. The branches lie about in all directions, and there is a carpet of twigs and leaves. In places, huge trunks rest against other trees. They have been torn out of their homes. The holes in the ground reek with the fumes of explosives. When the next rain falls they will be filled with water, and become dank and foul. The homes of the forest creatures, and even the creatures themselves have been blasted out of existence.

When all is quiet again, we continue the advance and come upon three German soldiers lying beside a hole in the ground. They have been killed by the bombs from their own aeroplanes. It is the price demanded by the Fatherland, but the Fatherland will never know and will never care about the hopes, the fears and the sufferings of these men and thousands of others like them.

Before we have gone far, the enemy's heavy artillery open out upon us. We cannot think how they have managed to spot us as the growth is so thick that we can only see a few yards ahead. Perhaps they only know that there are troops somewhere in the wood; their fire is not directed upon any particular spot. The 5.9's come shrieking in our direction. A lordly tree stops one of them, and groans as we hear the impact of the shell upon the trunk. There is a flash of fire, and the giant breaks above the half-way line and drops heavily to earth.

A second shell, and then a third, come towards us, and we know that a battery is engaged in the work of destruction. We sheer off to one side, in order to get away from the line of fire. Other troops run as we do – all searching for shelter. Someone finds a disused German trench and we all make for it. It is not deep, but it is fairly well protected. Large tree trunks have been dragged across it. We jump into it, and move farther along to make room for the other men. Again, we shall not come to any harm, unless a shell lands down upon us. If that were to happen, forty of us would be killed. But the chances are in our favour, and it is better than hiding in the undergrowth on the surface.

Each time a shell comes over, we get as low as possible in the trench. Even an inch might make a difference. Every time there is an explosion, the tree trunks vibrate like the strings of a musical instrument. Loose earth and dust descend upon us and make us cough. Then we brush ourselves, and know that we still live.

As the afternoon wears on, we go forward again. The Battalion has not lost many men: the bombs and shell-fire were more terrifying than destructive. The ground gained has been considerable.

Nothing further happens while we advance until we come to the edge of the wood. When it is ascertained that the Battalion is in line, we get the order to continue the attack. But before we have gone many yards, we see that we cannot move. On coming once more into the open, a storm of bullets descends upon us and we lose many men. The enemy are in strength ahead of us, and on emerging from the wood we are greeted with a fusillade of fire.

We go down immediately, and lie still. Then the order is passed along to retire to the edge of the wood and to take cover there. We pull ourselves back an inch at a time, and get behind bushes and young saplings. The Germans cannot see us, but we peep out so as to observe any movements ahead of us.

When evening comes we are still in the same position, as a

bigger effort than we are capable of making will be necessary to overcome the threatened resistance. The twilight is punctuated by shells which drop behind us. They burst among the trees, and the wood echoes like a tropical grassland when a lion roars out its challenge in the night.

The men on fatigue bring up our supper before night comes down upon us. They tell us that the Battalion field-kitchen has been brought right up into the wood, and that an excellent meal has been prepared for us. We gather around the large rectangular dixie, and fill our mess tins from it. Hot stew has been provided, as well as half a loaf of bread per man.

We sit on the ground behind the bushes, and dip our spoons into the stew. It contains chunks of meat and fat and pieces of potato. The gravy is appetising, and we do not waste a crumb of our bread ration. It is the first food that we have touched since the morning, and we are as hungry as jackals.

When the stew has disappeared, we fill our mess tins with tea. There is no opportunity to wash out our utensils, and grease floats in little blobs on the tea. But hungry men make little of such details.

The sugar in the tea partly takes away the taste of the stew. There is also cheese and biscuits for those who want them.

It is like a Sunday School picnic, and under other conditions we should enjoy ourselves. But in the wood, we just sit and munch our food and do not talk much. We are hungry and tired, and for all that we know, it may be the last meal that we shall ever eat.

During the night a Welsh Battalion comes up into the line. They sort themselves out and line the edge of the wood. We move back two hundred yards to make room for them, and sleep on the ground. The earth is soft and the fallen leaves give us comfortable beds.

There is nothing to keep up awake. We have been well fed, and the humus soil yields as we press our bodies into it. Besides, for the attack in the morning, we shall only act as support troops; the shock will fall upon the Welsh Battalion. They will cross the open field, and we shall follow them up, and only be called upon if they are held up. So with minds at rest, we drop off one by one.

Before dawn, the order comes to 'Stand to'. We rouse ourselves and rub our eyes; we seem to have scarcely slept at all. But the few hours of sleep have really done us much good, and we move forward to join the troops in the front line.

A few minutes before six the attack begins. Thousands of eyes peer out between the bushes and trees to see what lies in front. Then the shock troops go forward, and we move in to take their places.

There is no preliminary bombardment, possibly because our guns cannot fire through the wood effectively. The attackers rely on the element of surprise, and as they advance, only a little fire greets them. They cross the field and get behind a scrub hedge. This gives them good cover. The Lewis guns get into position, and a withering fire is directed upon a German trench a little farther on.

In ten minutes we see the attacking troops disappear behind the hedge. They rush the trench ahead of them with fixed bayonets. We cannot see what happens, but we hear a good deal of shouting. Then we leave the wood, and get into position behind the hedge.

The prisoners begin to come in. It is always the small men who appear to be given charge of them. Perhaps this is purely accidental, or it may be a preconcerted idea. It leaves the bigger men to continue the fighting, and so the attack gains more in frightfulness.

A group of eighteen prisoners passes by us. They are mostly young men. In charge of them are two bantams. One of them winks as he passes by, and says, 'A damn fine-looking lot of Jerries, aren't they?'

At a quarter-past-eight the advance is resumed. It is open country hereabouts, with a trench here and there. These are really only strong points, constructed to hold-up the advancing troops. A resolute enemy could bring an attack to a temporary standstill.

Our front-line troops work in sections. As one party is held up, another moves forward and brings enfilade fire to bear upon the defenders. There are few things so demoralizing as to find that the attacking troops are in rear of you. You have either to surrender, or die fighting.

The number of prisoners is considerable, though not large. A hundred or more have passed us since the early morning. Some of them have been carrying our own wounded. Four prisoners to one stretcher is the rule. They do not appear to mind this work. Perhaps it is because they are compelled to do it, and cannot refuse. Perhaps it is because they wish to put themselves right with their captors. Perhaps it is because they are glad to be on the side of the angels.

The quantity of shell-fire is not great. We know that the enemy have withdrawn their guns. A battery of heavies sends over an occasional salvo, but the shells do little damage. We hear them coming, and fling ourselves down. Then follows an explosion, and we know that the shells are falling two or three hundred yards from us.

If anyone is hit, the stretcher-bearers run to him and do all that is necessary. Then they call to some passing prisoners, and in this way the wounded are passed back to the field dressing-station. There they receive medical attention, and the usual injection against tetanus.

By nine o'clock, the attacking troops have advanced two miles.

Then the enemy are found in force, and in full daylight it would be useless to continue the attack without artillery support. They dig-in at all points.

Jerry is to be given no rest at all. He scarcely has a breathing space. No sooner has an attack died down than the next is in process of being planned or delivered. The sledge-hammer blows are being given at many points along the line, and he has no time to settle down. If he is given time, he becomes difficult to overcome. He tunnels in the ground like a badger, and has to be dug out patiently. If we catch him on the run, he is much less dangerous.

We go into the front line again. Our four Companies have been formed into two, in order that we shall be up to strength. The Welsh are in line with us, and on the other side is a battalion of Highlanders.

It seems that a competition is about to take place, to determine who can make the greatest distance in the shortest time; we do not mind who will win. What we do mind is that some of us will make a very long journey in a very short time, and we speculate upon our chances of getting through the next few days.

Behind us are the tanks. It is the first time that we have seen them. We have heard of them, and been told that they are irresistible. But we have not seen them in action, and are frankly sceptical. They have told us so many things that have not come to pass, that we merely look upon everything that we are told as something to encourage us. The spirit of the troops must be kept up, no matter how many souls are perjured.

The orders for the attack have been given clearly. There will not be any bombardment of the enemy's lines. We have come to rely more and more on the element of surprise. Sometimes it has answered tolerably well, and sometimes it has been a ghastly failure. On the whole, we prefer to deal with a pulverised enemy.

Shell-fire breaks their spirit, and gives us a better chance of coming through alive. If the surprise is complete, the attack usually succeeds. But Jerry is nearly always watchful, and he mans his trenches very quickly.

We wait in our positions, ready to go forward. We are like greyhounds straining at the leash. This is not because we wish to advance, but because we want to get it over.

When the night passes, the tanks break cover. They roar behind us, and in a few minutes we make room for them to pass us by. Some are large, and others are about half their size. The whippets are dotted diagonally in front of the bigger machines. As they thunder past us, we all cheer them on. They are heavily camouflaged and are terrifying to look at. They lurch from side to side but do not overturn. They plunge down a shell-hole, and climb out again on the other side. They give off petrol fumes that you could smell a mile away, and almost hide themselves in their own smoke. Nothing stands in their way, and we know when they pass us that at last we have produced a weapon that will the win the war. Neither man nor devil could withstand these things. The caterpillar wheels crush barbed wire as though it were string. The inmates are protected by steel which is inches thick. Given a sufficient number of tanks, we would go from end to end of Europe, driving the enemy before us.

When the tanks are twenty yards ahead of us, we follow them up. They move quickly, and we have to trot to keep pace with them. So that we do not expose ourselves, we keep behind them. Crossing No-man's-land like this does not worry us at all. It is the safest passage that we have ever made.

The whippets lead the way to knock out the machine-gun nests. They carry small artillery as well as Lewis guns. There is nothing so effective to deal with the enemy; small-arms ammunition just bounces off their armour plate.

In a few minutes we have made three hundred yards without a

casualty. Then the enemy's gun-fire begins. The whizz-bangs shriek as they pass us. It is difficult for Jerry's guns to get the range of a moving object. Besides, the tanks do not move in a straight line. They avoid large obstacles as much as possible, then curl inwards again to keep their position in relation to the other tanks.

Forty yards away a tank is hit by a 5.9 shell. The shell bursts with a more than usual roar. The crash of metal on metal, the flash of fire, and the explosion all happen together. As the smoke clears away, we see the tank lying on its side. Its caterpillar wheels continue to revolve. They clutch at the air like a giant in rigor mortis. The engine roars in protest. Two men, hatless, jump out, and inspect the gaping wound in its side.

We move on to the attack. The tank covering us veers off to the left, and its Lewis gun comes into action. We guess that it is dealing with a machine-gun nest, and do not interrupt it in its work. It fires three bursts and then accelerates.

We pass over the enemy. There are seven of them and two machine-guns. Two of the Jerries have been pressed right into the earth, and are exactly level with the surface of the ground. One gun is broken into small pieces. The other men just lie on the ground beside their gun. They have finished with the war and with the world. In passing them, we see on their faces a stricken look, such as is seen on the faces of all things that are hunted.

Shells fall all along the line. The enemy's artillery make rapid fire to try to hold up the tanks. It is in answer to the SOS signal from the infantry. But the tanks are relentless. They dodge about, and make for any troops who show themselves. When they get near to them, the engines roar out defiance, and the machine-guns in the tanks really come into their own. The noise is like that of hailstones falling on a tin roof in a tropical storm.

The advancing infantry act only as snipers, to deal with any whom the tanks miss. One man is hardly worth attention from them. They just pass him by as they lumber forward in search of more worthwhile prey.

A batch of prisoners passes us. They continue to hold up their hands until they are out of sight. There is no-one in charge of them, but they are unarmed, and would not, in any case, come back again. Before they have gone far, someone will take charge of them, and march them off to the collecting stations.

The front line and the supporting line are captured in good time. Nothing holds us up, and we go on and on. A battery of field guns fires from a coppice near by. But the tanks are inexorable. Two of them rake the gun team with Lewis gun fire. We see three gunners fall; then the others surrender. They wear steel hats, resting well down over the ears. Some of them are big men. Beside their guns are small stacks of shells. The guns are camouflaged in the same way as our own field-guns; the barrels are painted like the poles outside barbers' shops. I think of Polly and recall that it was guns like these that gave us hell in the sunken road. Now it is our turn.

Our tank slackens speed and finally comes to a standstill. We remain beside it and await further orders. On either side of us the action continues, and the noise of the rifles and machine-guns, mingles with the roar of the engines. The battlefield smells like a garage.

Stretcher-bearers run at the double. The Red Cross men attend to a wounded Tommy, then put the body onto a stretcher, and double away to another man who has fallen. A second stretcher-case is carried away. The enemy's shell-fire ploughs up the earth.

We sit on the ground behind the tank and take out some food from our haversacks. Water-bottles are passed round. We gargle, rather than swallow the water.

Gradually, the noises die down, and the tanks waddle back one by one. They have smashed their way through the German line. We remain to hold on to the ground that has been won. It is the least expensive frontal attack that we have known.

In the afternoon an artillery officer and some men arrive. They inspect the battery of captured field guns, and remove some parts from them. We guess that this is to prevent the enemy using them against us again, should he succeed in recapturing them.

The rest of the day is our own. We just lie about and smoke and talk. The more curious ones among us go and inspect the quarters of the German artillery men. They have made themselves comfortable by using a natural fold in the ground, not far from their guns. It has been deepened and blocked-up at both ends to form a trench-cum-dug-out. Sheets of zinc and piles of earth rest upon the top. Jerry always makes a home for himself wherever he goes. He is adept at making himself as comfortable as possible even on the battlefield. His deeper dug-outs are models of ingenuity.

Black bread and some cigars are found. We taste them, but do not like them. If such rations were issued to us we should not accept them. But perhaps we do not believe as sincerely in the righteousness of our cause as do the German soldiers. Or it may be that we are not by birth or training a military nation, and not accustomed to such Spartan fare. The black bread is hard: it is many days old. Also, to us, it is unsightly. It looks coarse, and tastes like sawdust. It may be capable of supporting life, but not the kind of life to which we are accustomed.

The cheroots burn and taste like brown paper. We do not wonder why Jerry looks grateful to us when we share our cigarettes or tobacco with him. It is probably the only decent smoke he has had since coming to the Front. The enemy must think that we live like lords on the fat of the land. They look upon our bully-beef, pork and beans, and fine white bread as food fit for the gods.

These things convince us that at least some of the stories which we have heard contain a measure of truth. If the troops in the line are kept on poor rations, conditions in Germany must indeed be bad. We have only to hang on, and in time the enemy will crack up even if we do not attack them.

The Battle of Fresnoy-le-Petit, another battle of the Hindenburg Line has ended disastrously for the Germans. It has yielded them naught for their comfort.

CHAPTER TWELVE

Farewell, Bill

Bill Washbrook and I stumble along in the darkness. Behind us, the Very lights go up. Yellow balls light up the night. Jerry is nervous and keeps on sending up his flares every five minutes. But we scarcely think about them as we have finished with such things for a while.

We move further away from the line as our Battalion has been relieved. There are no guides; we must find our own way back. That is why we stumble along over ploughed lands and through long grass. The night is dark, and we are dog-tired and have no means of knowing where we are going. We only know that we are heading for the rear and shall be out of the maelstrom for a little while. It is enough to know just that.

In front of us our artillery pound the enemy. We see the flash of the guns, and the shells pass high above us. They have been aimed at the transport and the roads behind the German lines. We judge that the guns are eight-inch howitzers at least. They have a savage bark. Four sheets of flame follow in quick succession, and the massive shells hurtle high into the sky.

By day and by night Jerry is harried by our guns. They strafe him for half-an-hour many times a day. The objects are to destroy his morale and to silence his batteries.

We trudge alone and are almost overcome by weariness. Our boots become heavier and heavier. When we reach the gun pits we decide to go no further. One place is as good as another to us for the rest of the night.

For a few minutes we watch the gunners. They all have their coats off, and work with a powerful torch. An officer gives them the range and direction. Then they elevate or depress the guns. Everything is based upon angles. I am fascinated by the apparent simplicity of the method.

My reverie is broken by the command, 'Fire!' All four guns in the Battery send over another salvo. I wonder about the beautiful parabolas which we used to discuss in the sixth form, as the shells make their way over the enemy lines.

The gunners sweat at their jobs. The shells are heavy, and have first to be raised from the ground on to a platform. Then they are put into the breach and rammed home. The guns recoil and we cannot hear anything for several minutes following the percussion.

When the gunners finish their 'shoot', they receive their ration of hot tea and rum. They give us a share, and we think ourselves lucky. The artillery men never fail to be considerate to the infantry. Whenever they can do them a good turn, it seems to give them satisfaction. We have no better friends.

Bill and I decide to sleep where we are; we cannot go on walking all the night. Our feet have begun to give us trouble as we have not had our boots off for four days. So we sit on the ground and remove them, while the gunners go to their quarters fifty yards away until it is time to fire off another dozen rounds.

We are only two miles behind the Front, and wear our gas masks at the alert. The satchels rest upon our chests, and we open and turn back the flaps. Then we each light a cigarette, stretch oursleves flat on our backs, and smoke. When the cigarettes are finished, we loosen the necks of our tunics, turn over on our sides, curl up like wood lice, and go to sleep.

The night is not cold and we sleep soundly. We are dead beat. But before we have been asleep long, I am awakened. The enemy batteries are searching for our artillery. The shells come over four at a time, at intervals of a few seconds. They are high-explosive shells and burst like 5.9's. We lie on the slope of a hill. The shells fall just behind us, and the crash is deafening.

Bill sleeps through two salvos. Before the third, I turn over and wake him. He is quite played out and full of sleep, and merely grunts and says, 'What the bloody hell?' and goes off again. It is high time that he got away from the Front. For some weeks, and particularly at meal times, I have noticed that his hands have been shaking like those of a person who has Parkinson's disease.

I pull on my boots. Another whine tells me that the enemy has no intention of giving us any rest. The ground shakes, and chunks of steel go hurtling through the air and crash against pieces of corrugated iron. The night is made hideous. Some of the pieces come in our direction and I hear the thud as they go into the earth near us. Any one of them would go clean through us. They are as sharp as splintered glass, and hot and buzzing.

We are totally helpless in the darkness. I rouse Bill again, and though he is only half awake, I persuade him that we must move immediately. There is nowhere for us to go where we may be safe, so we just run into the night. We run anywhere, thinking only of getting away from the shell-fire.

The fourth salvo catches us. We run right into it. So that we may not lose each other, we grasp hands. When the shell is a long way off we hear it coming. It cleaves the air like an express train, and each second the sound becomes more ominous. We know that our time has come. You cannot be lucky forever at the Front. But it is too bad to be caught like this so far behind the line.

It crashes down like a meteorite out of the skies, and lifts us clean off the ground. We fall upon our faces and are bruised all over. The fumes nearly choke us. I hold my breath, sniff, and shout out 'Gas!' And then I hold my breath again and fight for life. Three seconds is the time allowed for pulling one's respirator out of the satchel and putting it on. I have often done it within the time, while training in England and in the trenches.

I pull the bag over my head, and tuck it in round the bottom. The neck of my tunic is unhooked. Then I find the mouth-piece, and breathe through it. My breath comes in short gasps, and my heart thumps wildly. The taste and smell of chemicals nearly sickens me. I splutter and feel faint, but know that it would be suicidal to throw off the gas mask.

It is so dark that I can see nothing at all through the goggles. They become damp, and would be almost entirely useless even on a starlit night. The hot air which I breathe out causes a mist to form upon them.

I hear Bill coughing and go to him. He tells me that he knows that he is gassed. His gas helmet is only half on, and I fear that he has not been quick enough. His hands shake as though he is sick of the palsy. I finish off the job for him, but I know that the Boches have got him at last. He coughs and splutters and chokes.

We move on again, hand in hand. Fear lends us wings, and we walk and walk, not knowing and not caring where we go. We make frequent pauses, and sometimes sit on the ground to recover our wind. Our faces stream with perspiration and the respirators become worse each moment. Three hours is the time for which they can be worn in comfort. That is what the text books laid down. Three minutes nearly kill us, and we feel as though we are being suffocated. But we dare not remove them. If we were to do so, we should not get far: the Front is drenched in gas. We have been caught. The first salvos were all high explosives and shrapnel. The deception has paid off.

We can go no farther. Bill is entirely played-out, so we agree to stop. Someone hears us talking, and calls out to us to come into shelter. We crawl into a small tunnel in an embankment more dead than alive. A wet blanket covers the entrance to it.

I pull off my respirator, put my water-proof sheet over my head, and my hands into my pockets. The place swarms with rats. But my skin is protected, and I soon fall asleep.

When morning comes I am awakened by the sound of coughing. It is dark in the tunnel, and I decide to move out into the light. I try to take my hands out of my pockets, in order to throw off the ground-sheet. I cry out in agony. I cannot move my arms. It occurs to me that the cramped position in which I have slept is responsible. So I try a second time, but again without success. Then I know that it is not cramp that will not allow me to move.

I shout for help, and someone comes. He removes the water-proof sheet from around my head, and dimly I see a glimmer of light. I ask the time, and am told that it has just turned six o'clock.

My eyes ache terribly. I hope that it is because they have not become accustomed to the darkness. Subconsciously, I know that there is another reason for it, but I am loath to admit the possibility to myself.

My rescuer asks me what is the matter. I tell him that my hands are in my pockets, and that I cannot take them out. He tugs at one arm and I cry out loudly. The pain is intense. Then, with his jack-knife, he rips up the sides of my trousers. My arms fall limply out of them.

We move out into the open. The coughing increases in volume, and the glare of the morning light causes me to blink wildly. I cannot see at all with the left eye. The right one lets in a pin-prick of light.

Around me there are nearly a hundred men. Some are standing, some are sitting, some are kneeling and some are lying. Many of them are already dead. They strew the ground like planks tossed up on a beach by an angry sea. They cough and vomit and retch. They fight to the end, and quantities of yellowish-green matter come out of their mouths. The mucus seems to be a yard or more in length and is thick. They toss about and fling themselves over and over in the most tremendous agony. Their eyes roll and some of them swear terrifically. The groaning must be heard a mile away. Beside them there are pools which look like stagnant water, and they are covered with blood and mucus. In a few more hours half of these badly gassed men will be dead. The once peaceful meadow has become a graveyard.

Red Cross orderlies rush about. In their hands they carry bottles. They pass by those for whom no help is possible, and attend to the less serious cases. Often times they know that they can do no good. For a half of us no restorative has any value. The worst cases are beyond all human help.

Bill can still sit up. He coughs without ceasing, and retches as though he will bring up the entire contents of his thorax. Everything that he spits out is yellowish-green in colour and viscous. His face has aged ten years in a night. He sees me through a mist of tears, and beckons me to come to him. I make my way across, and we sit down together. All the laughter has gone out of life for us. I know that Bill has only a few hours of life left to him.

I am rapidly becoming blind. The light of day hurts terribly, and my eyes feel full of sand. It is as though someone has thrown a handful of sand into each of them. They burn like two red-hot coals. The little light which pierces them becomes rapidly less.

The upper part of my body feels as though it has been roasted. My shirt does not want to leave me; it clings tenaciously, and the weight of it is almost insupportable. I have discarded my tunic because it was too heavy to wear. I cannot raise my arms. They feel as though they are made of lead, and hurt frightfully if I try to move them. They just lie at my sides and burn.

Someone takes my hand. I do not know who he is, but at the Front it is like that. We travel down the road together. He tells me when we go carefully to cross a ditch or shell-hole and tugs me by the arm to avoid running into obstacles like trees and stones. I support him when he has a bout of coughing and choking. His lungs are in bad shape and he will be lucky if he survives many days. We stagger along like two very drunk men.

We are divided into two classes. The dead do not count. They will be buried where they lie, or one large pit will be dug for them. Then they will be collected and piled into it. Among the living there are stretcher cases and walking cases. All those who do not vomit continuously, are walking cases. The others are spared all exertion, and have to be carried.

We stream down the road in a procession. It is not a ceremonial parade. There is no 'quick march' or 'knees up', as we once learnt on the parade ground. We are not in alignment, nor are we dressed from the right. We only go as quickly as we are able to travel. Our buttons do not shine. Our chins are all unshaven. We bear no resemblance to troops who have humbled the enemy. We are more ragged than the gamins of any continental town as we make our way to the dressing-station at a snail's pace. Perhaps there will be some help for us at the end of another half mile.

Stretcher-bearers pass us on their return journey. Sometimes they do not manage to reach the dressing-station. They leave the corpse by the roadside and go back in search of someone else who needs their help.

They do not keep us long at the dressing-station. Two doctors are at work, and several men help them. One of the orderlies tries to remove my shirt. The skin comes away in large patches, and I feel it leaving me. It is like having parts of oneself torn away. The orderly takes a pair of scissors and cuts the shirt to pieces. Then he smears my body with oil, and wraps yards of cloth all round me. It eases the pain, but I feel like a trussed-up chicken.

My head is swathed in bandages, and day has been changed into night. I only know that the sun is shining because I feel the warmth of it. I live in utter darkness.

When the doctors have examined us, clerks fill in all the particulars, and we are given little tickets like labels. On them is written our Name, Regimental Number, Religion, Nature of Wound, and other necessary information. These labels are tied to the buttons of our tunics. Mine is fastened round my neck and hangs like a lady's pendant.

Then we are assisted into motor ambulances. They stand outside the dressing-station. The engines are kept ticking over so that no time is lost. When each is full it starts off down the road.

In our ambulance there are lying cases and sitting cases. Two orderlies attend to us. The driver drops into low gear when he comes to a particularly bad stretch of road. Each time the wheels strike a bump, we cry out in pain. We cannot help doing so.

When any man becomes sick, the orderlies attend to him. They are inexpressibly sorry for us, and do everything for our comfort. If we shift our positions when the ambulance lurches, they handle us with great care. They are as gentle as hospital nurses and most efficient. I recognise the West Country burr as they converse together.

My body feels on fire. The skin is all sizzled, and the bandages keep in the heat. It is like nitric acid acting upon copper. I am being eaten away. The nerves in my skin are all affected: the shock to the system is great. An orderly gives me tablets to swallow to ease the pain. They contain morphia, and I feel drowsy. But I only sleep intermittently. When the car swings or lurches I half-wake and then doze off again.

In the bunk above me is a lung case. He coughs all the time. He twists and turns, and hangs half out of his bed to seek relief. He vomits into a dish which is held up to his mouth. I am too insensible to feel squeamish. But I am more fortunate than he is, as my lungs do not appear to be affected in any way, while he seems to be eaten away inwardly.

In front of us and behind us are other ambulances. We hear the engines as though in a dream, and know that these ambulances are full of other cases like ourselves, coming down from the Front.

At last we pull up and the driver tells us that we have reached our destination. Orderlies lift us out of the ambulance, and we lie upon our stretchers on the ground. In turn, we are taken into the Medical Officer's tent and placed on a table. He glances at my label and directs the orderlies to take me to a particular tent. Again I am carried, and again placed on the ground. Then a doctor and male nurse wait upon me. They examine me, and speak in technical terms which are only intelligible to the trained person. Here and there I understand a word. I see now why all the sciences have a language of their own. If it were not so, we should know too much about ourselves, and that would be disquieting.

CHAPTER THIRTEEN

Hospital Interlude

Twenty-five miles behind the Front, two men undress and put me into bed. It is the first time in my life that I have had a man to look after me. I have often wondered what it would be like to have a valet, but never thought that the opportunity would come my way.

I have not slept in a bed for many months. There are clean sheets and a real pillow. The bed is a simple iron stretcher, but very comfortable. It gives a little, when I try to turn over to ease myself. Or this may be due to the pneumatic mattress under me.

I do not know if I run a temperature or not, although I feel on fire, but I am put on to invalid diet. Hot milk, rice pudding, bread and milk, beef-tea, cornflour, jelly, barley broth, tinned peaches and thin cream are my fare. I do not want anything else, and often do not want even these tempting delicacies. The peaches and thin cream are perhaps the pick of the lot.

The nurse often comes to see me, and tries to persuade me to eat. My arms are quite useless to me: they lie like two dead branches. To move them is torture. My neck and chest are raw and charred and feel wet and hot. I have become like a little child, and depend for my sustenance on those around me. They feed me with a spoon and a drinking-cup. Everything is held up to my mouth.

Once a day my bandages are unwrapped. The doctor comes around at ten o'clock in the morning. He personally supervises the removal of my wrappings, and helps the nurse to attend to my eyes. I do not know what they do, but they pour something into them. It feels like oil, and is deliciously cool and soothing. But the heat in my eyes is terrific, and almost unbearable. The eyelids are quite shut, and all the time they feel as though they have been roasted. I cannot see anything, and even if I were able to open my eyes, I should not want to do so. They are like a very small baby – they ask only to be protected.

The skin on my neck and face and body has become all wrinkled; it is in ridges and furrows. Even the weight of my pyjamas presses heavily. I lie inert like a log, not daring to turn on to either side. It would be easier for me if I could turn over, as the pressure on my back would then be relieved.

There are cases of all descriptions in our tent. Most of us are gas cases and we hardly know a quiet moment. Men cough and retch all day long, and the nurses and orderlies run from one to another to support the worst cases. Some of them struggle hard to get out of bed, although they know that any exertion affects the heart. But they cannot help themselves; they only want relief, and resort to any means to obtain it.

On one side of me is a man with bullet wounds in the left leg. He was hit while going across No-man's-land during an attack. A burst of machine-gun fire caught him and smashed his thigh. He cannot move his leg, and to keep him quiet, he is given a large amount of medicine. It probably contains morphia or bromide; he knows that when he is fit to travel he will be marked for England. The Army has no further use for him. Nearly every day he asks the Sergeant if he can go down the line with the next draft. His turn will probably come soon. He tells me that this is the third time he has been wounded.

On the other side is a shrapnel case. His right arm and shoulder have been hit in three places. He thinks that with luck he will have finished with the war, and there is nothing he wants so much as to get home again.

The worst case in our tent is that of a shell-shocked man. He is not the most dangerously ill, but we doubt if he will ever get well again. He was blown up by an enemy shell during an attack upon the trench which he was helping to defend. During the daytime he lies quietly in his bed and has very little to say to anyone. At night, he is a source of worry to us all, and often wakes us out of our sleep. Without any warning whatever, he suddenly springs up in his bed and shouts at the top of his voice, 'They are coming over! They are coming over!' For a few minutes he goes clean out of his mind, and the orderlies run and hold him down. We do not know if he would become violent and cause somebody an injury; but he might injure himself. He scarcely seems to know what is happening, and goes on shouting, 'They are coming over!' Then he gradually subsides, falls back, sighs deeply, and relapses into semi-consciousness. This happens two and sometimes even three times in a night. It is impossible for him to control his terrible nightmares.

We do not see how he will ever get well again. The shell-shock has utterly destroyed his nerves. He lives in a world apart from us, and sees a host of field-grey uniforms coming over the top to attack him. We see in him a case of mental conflict; the unity of mind has been destroyed. The ego is in danger, and has sought an advantage of flight into neurosis. He is anxious for his safety, and his anxiety has developed a tremendous intensity. The ego pays heavily for the solution of the conflict. His soul is in agony.

Psycho-analysis might do something for him, but he may not have the good fortune to be able to get the right treatment. Life is worse than death to him. He comes out in a cold sweat each time the dread comes upon him. When the attack has worked itself out, he falls back exhausted.

The sister in charge of our tent makes time every day to come and talk to me. I cannot see her, but the other men tell me that I am lucky. Everybody loves her and would do anything for her. She is quiet and very efficient. It is clear to all of us that she has undertaken work which is not her usual work. I am saddened that such a nice person should see all around her so much man-made tragedy, and spend every day dealing with us human wrecks. I tell her so, but she replies that she is happy in helping us all. She speaks a language which I have not heard spoken for a long time. The language spoken by men in the trenches has its own peculiar qualities; it is forceful and expressive, but crude. The sister has a pleasing voice; it is neither high nor low, and the timbre is clear and mellow. She is evidently well-educated and has probably had lessons in voice control. She talks effortlessly. There is no striving after effect, and she is not pedantic. She chooses her words carefully, and always says the correct word to indicate the correct shade of meaning.

She is almost run off her legs with work. When there is spare time, she sits on my bed, although it is against the rules, and talks to me. English poetry is often the subject. She quotes lines from Chaucer, Keats, Shakespeare and other great masters of the language. Then she goes off again to attend to her duties. Each evening, before going off duty, she brings me a glass of hot milk and a biscuit. She sometimes comes in to see me at night. I only know that she has come when she says, 'Would you like some peaches and cream?' At times she varies it with 'Would you like some jelly?' I wish that it was possible to see her. The other fellows say that she is under thirty years of age, a red-head, and very good-looking.

We are on our way to the Base. It only took two days for the Red Cross sergeant to arrange it. With me are the two men in the beds next to mine. I am the poorer by a pocket watch, but consider that I have got off lightly.

The medical officer in charge of the wounded passes along from one carriage to another. He stops to attend to the urgent cases. He is accompanied by nurses and the RAMC sergeant. A Sister is in charge of each compartment. We are all cared for as if each one of us was a patient in a private ward in a well-run hospital. Everybody is most attentive to our needs.

We swing along through the night and other trains rush past us. They are taking troops back to the line. In a day or two many of them will be coming down again. And some will never make the return journey.

At a station we pull up for breakfast and wait for an hour or more. The jolting in the train has caused my temperature to rise again, and I am given only hot milk and a biscuit. But I do not want to eat anything. I sip the milk out of the drinking cup; it has a spout like a teapot.

The engine jerks, chains clank, and we move on again. These train drivers are the worst in the world. From the time the trains begin to move, it is five minutes before they get properly on their way. The bumps are passed from carriage to carriage, and nearly shake us out of our bunks. As we proceed, most of us fall asleep or doze off if possible. There is nothing else for us to do. I cannot see the countryside, and do not know what is going on around me. The noise of the wheels drowns all sounds except the groans of the badly wounded men.

In the afternoon a fleet of ambulances meets the train. We are all taken out of our bunks and carried to the cars. They rattle along the cobbled streets and climb out of the town.

We are in a real hospital at Trouville. It is purely a war-time hospital, and consists of huts built of wood. They are lined inside with asbestos, and are clean and extremely comfortable. There are twenty beds on each side of our ward, and two large stoves down the centre. Iron chimneys pass upwards through the roof. There is a locker behind every bed, and I am reminded of the dormitory at school. The stoves keep us warm all day and all night. There is no shortage of coal; orderlies and men on light duty fill the buckets whenever they are empty. There is a huge coal yard about a quarter of a mile away where they go to get it. German prisoners are on duty at the coal yard; they unload all the trucks that come in, and shovel the coal into the buckets when required to do so.

Our doctor is a Canadian. I cannot see him, but everybody in the ward says that he is a good sort. Some of the patients have been down the line for months, and have had ample time to get to know him. He is a man over sixty, and very grey. He is as kindly a person as can be imagined. He has never been known to hurry a man out of hospital. He will not mark you fit until you are really fit and ready to be discharged to return to the Front. In this respect he is almost unique.

I do not know anything about his skill, but his kindliness more than makes up for many other things. He limps badly, and I am told that this is the result of a shrapnel wound received in the line at Ypres in 1915. This alone would be sufficient to account for his treatment to us. He has seen things for himself, and knows that a half-fit man is an encumbrance in the trenches. Somebody else always has to do his work, and life there is strenuous enough if each man does his own task and is not called upon to do a task and a half.

The MO spends a long time in examining me. He gives me a thorough overhaul, as though he is interested in his work, and seeks to do the best for himself and for me. He speaks quietly and is unhurried. He is a very gentle man and not brusque. I feel that I could not be in better hands, and trust him implicitly.

The removal of the bandages round my body is too painful and I cannot stand it. The skin and the flesh come away with the cloth. The doctor sees that I am terribly burnt, and the nurses do not continue to pull off the bandages. The sheets are put back into position again. I lie exhausted.

Then he examines my eyes. I am still stone-blind and am unable to see anything. My ears alone tell me whether it is the doctor or the nurse who speaks. The daylight hurts, and the fierce burning sensation has not abated. The doctor remarks, 'Hmm . . . mustard gas!' I reply, 'I do not know, sir, but I think so'.

We sit on the bed together although it is against the rules of the hospital. That is largely why everybody in the ward loves this man. He is unconventional and friendly. He does not stand on ceremony. He calls me 'Sonny' and treats me as a friend. He asks me to tell him where and how I was gassed. I tell him that it was on the St Quentin front, and two or three miles behind the line at night. He puts his hand on my shoulder and says, 'We will see what can be done'. He talks about the gas attack at Ypres in '15 when the Hun sent over the deadly chlorine and caught the Canadians and Zouaves.

His words and his behaviour make me feel better. I know that he is intensely sorry for me, and will do his utmost to make me well again. I feel instinctively that his utmost will be a good effort and a prolonged effort. In the afternoon, the Sister, some nurses and the doctor come to me. They put the screens round my bed, and hide me from the view of the other men in the ward. The chattering dies down to a whispering, and in a few minutes even that ceases. The patients have become accustomed to such sights as they occur almost daily.

Under the doctor's directions, all the upper part of my body is soaked in oil. It eases the pain and helps to loosen the bandages. A little cloth is cut away here and there, where it hangs loosely. Nothing is pulled off. The only thing to do is to play a waiting game, and to make me as comfortable as possible in the meantime.

The days succeed one another. Each day is like the previous one. The ward wakes up at five o'clock in the morning. Nurses and orderlies begin to wash the patients at that hour. There is always a considerable amount of grumbling, as the men do not see the necessity for being awakened so early. They all feel that they have weeks and months of sleep to make up, and they could gladly sleep on until ten in the morning. As each man is washed, he turns over and drops off to sleep again until breakfast is brought in.

At half-past seven we have our first meal. It is brought to us on trays. Walking cases help as much as possible with all the meals and also with making the beds. Some of them do it from a sense of duty; some hope that by making themselves useful they may get a soft job on the Staff; others find that it pays to make frequent incursions into the kitchen. Nearly always there are some tit-bits to be found there. Certain fellows have a good nose for tinned salmon, herrings in tomato sauce, and trifle and tea to follow.

After nine o'clock the doctor makes his rounds. By ten, he has finished with our ward, and then we have our morning tea. Within limits we can make our own choice. Tea, hot milk and beef tea are provided, and each man receives two biscuits. We take them whether we need them or not. This is like the laws of the Medes and Persians. Somebody can do with them, and if we did not take them they would only go to fatten other people who have no need of them. We have not seen such good fare for many months, and have almost forgotten about it. It is like being back in civilian life once more.

From eleven until twelve the men do all kinds of things. Some sleep, some write letters, some play cards, some help the nurses with medicines, and some sit beside the fire and talk. There is no lack of things to talk about.

At twelve, the mid-day meal is brought round, and from two until four is the recognised rest time. Talking is forbidden, but reading and writing are permitted.

Three evenings a week we are entertained, provided there is nobody in the ward who cannot stand noise. Concert parties visit the hospital and the members pass from one ward to another. They sing, tell stories, recite and practise sleight-of-hand tricks.

Every second day I have a fresh dressing put on my body. Cotton wool soaked in oil is kept in position with bandages. Each day my eyes receive attention, but apart from the lessening of the burning sensation, they seem to be no better. The bandages are changed each day, and the MO makes his examination daily. He asks what life is like in the front line trenches these days, and shows a real interest in me. I respect him and even become very fond of this humane man.

Perhaps it is his cheerfulness that prevents me from becoming despondent. I scarcely ever think of blindness. The future does not worry me in the least. I am still too young to know that seventy years is a very long time. I am well developed physically, but mentally I am still a child. Time, as well as experience is needed to make us quite grown-up.

Or perhaps my attitude is a fatalistic one, not common to youths of my age, but thrust upon me by living at the Front. In the trenches we were powerless to alter our environment to any great extent; we just took what came, and believed that what is to be, will be. It is a common philosophy of soldiers, and without it, life would soon become unbearable. It has often kept us going when in the line.

Any amount of anxiety would not help me in the least. I must just wait and see what will happen. My lungs have not been burnt out, and whatever the worst may be that will befall me, I shall go on living. I think of Polly and Bill, and decide that it is better to live as a blind man than to die from stomach wounds or poison gas as they did. If the worst comes to the worst, I shall still have music and the song of birds, and kind friends will read to me the accounts of county cricket matches. Besides these things, I have a home to which I may return, and nobody will be dependent upon me. And I have the best parents in the whole wide world who will always care for me and protect me.

In due course, the doctor decides to remove the bandages from my eyes. The first day, the light of the sun, though not bright, hurts them. The second day, I am able to see a little light through the left eye. The eyelid quivers as though it is undecided whether to open or close. After a minute the bandages are put on again.

Each day the practice is repeated, and only after twelve days does the right eye show any signs of response to treatment. The time of exposure is lengthened each day, and at the end of another week I am without bandages for twenty minutes a day. By dint of much squinting I am able for the first time to see my fellow patients.

One of them is a particularly interesting case. He is a South African boy, about twenty-two years old, and he has been in hospital for nearly a year. His face is terribly mutilated. I hesitate to look at him, both out of respect for his own feelings and because the sight almost frightens me. A deep furrow begins over the left eye and runs right along the forehead. Then it goes down one cheek, across the mouth, and half-way up the other cheek. It is deep and is a total disfigurement.

When we are on speaking terms I ask him what happened. He tells me that somewhere north of the River Somme he ran into liquid fire, and was left for dead on the field. Two days later he was picked up by stretcher-bearers and carried back.

He is one of the nicest fellows I have met – quiet and unassuming. He tells me that he thinks that the wound will enable him to get his discharge, if only because of its effects upon the morale of other troops. In the ward he has been given light duty to do, pending the decision of the Medical Board.

One morning a strange doctor comes into our ward. He asks if we will volunteer to go out, as a large convoy of badly wounded men is expected in the hospital that evening. Many of us are far from well, but every one of us volunteers to make room for those who are worse off than ourselves. In the afternoon we are taken to a convalescent camp not far away. Some of us have to return to the ward each day for further treatment. We also collect any letters and parcels for ourselves and all the others.

When I go back the following day, I find the ward full to overflowing. They all appear to be shrapnel cases. I look through the door to see if the Sister is free to attend to me, and see that every bed is occupied. Many of the men have head wounds, and the bandages are still soaked in blood. There are middle-aged men, young men, and mere boys. They all look ghastly, and the worst cases are as bad as anything that I have ever seen. It is clear that a good number of them will only leave the ward as corpses. The others will be in hospital for many months.

One the tops of the lockers I notice several small German hats. They have different-coloured ribbons and little buttons on them. I wonder why our men have troubled to bring such souvenirs down the line as they are counted of little value in the trenches. The Sister tells me that all the casualties are German troops, and that a whole train load has come into the hospital.

The sight gladdens and sickens me. I can see that our artillery have been giving the Jerries hell. They will not stand up to that treatment very long. Shells, and still more shells is the only way to end the war. The quicker the casualties mount-up, the sooner will the war be over. The sad thing is that it should have to happen, in order that a few Generals may make a name for themselves.

My comrades in the convalescent camp are furious that we have been inveigled out of the ward to make room for wounded Jerries. There is much to be said for their argument, as some of them are far from fit, and would not normally have been discharged from hospital for another month or more. I point out to them that the poor devils need treatment even more than we do, but I have little faith in my own argument. We all feel aggrieved because we have been tricked. It is doubtful if any of us would have volunteered to leave the hospital if we had known who were the badly wounded men.

Our Canadian doctor would not have treated us in that way. But there is nothing left for us to do except to make the most of the situation.

Life in the convalescent camp has one big advantage over life in the hospital. We have fresh fruit every day. Some of it is obtained honestly, in the form of presents. But most of it is stolen fruit. Apples and pears are to be found in the orchards a mile or two away. Our men go there two or three times a week, and come back laden. They take pillow-slips with them, and hide them inside their blue jackets. One orchard is alongside a main road and the convalescent men often go that way for walks. They fill their pillow-slips, and bring them back to the huts under cover of darkness.

On Sunday afternoons we are allowed to have visitors from three till five o'clock. The French civilians come to see us. I have made friends with a whole family. Charlotte, the youngest, is fifteen years old. She acts as our interpreter. Her command of English is better than my command of French. Charlotte's mother comes too; her father is a Captain in the French army and is fighting at Verdun. The grandfather and grandmother do not speak any English, but the old gentleman is a retired sea-captain, and knows the coastline near my home in Cornwall, near Land's End. He tells me the names of several lighthouses, and beams when I say that I know them well. This gives us a starting point for our friendship. Other members of the party are Marie Louise and her mother. They are refugees from the Ardennes.

Every Sunday all these people come to see me, and they always bring a basketful of food. There is always a large bunch of grapes and a bottle of wine, besides cigars and French rolls. They gather round my bed as though I am a son of the family, and fire all kinds of questions at me. They want to know what life is like in the front line; if I have killed any Germans, and if so, how many? How much longer do I think the war will last? What is my opinion of the French soldiers as fighters? – and so on. It becomes clear to me that the French and the British people have a very different attitude towards the Germans. We kill them because for the time being they are opposed to us. The French kill them because they consider them as vermin, and not fit to live. They look upon them as Huns and Vandals and inferior beings. I am forced to the conclusion that they are hereditary enemies, and that there will never be any real peace between them. The old sea-captain's eyes flash fire as he speaks of the Jerries. He always calls them '*les Boches*' and '*les canailles*'. He talks like a machine-gun; it is always rapid fire.

Marie Louise and her mother tell me that they were forced to leave their home in the Ardennes when the Uhlans came riding like conquerors through their village, as well as other places in their neighbourhood. They speak nostalgically about the beauty of the forests and deep valleys and their eyes fill with tears as they tell me their story. They fear that everything which they have lived for will be despoiled and laid waste. All the people retired, taking only what they could carry away from their homes.

When I become stronger and am able to walk a little distance, my French friends ask me to come to their house to dinner. Two of us are invited. Palmer, an artillery signalman in the next bed, is asked to come with me. We are not able to obtain a pass to stay out late, so we decide to chance our luck and go without permission to absent ourselves. We cut across the fields and dodge along the side streets, avoiding the military police. By careful inquiry, we know exactly where they may be found.

The dinner party is a jolly little affair. Subdued electric lights and candles give the room a welcoming look. There is the gleam of china and cut glass. We have almost forgotten about the amenities of civilization, and have to think twice before we decide which knives and forks to use. It becomes necessary to unlearn many of the things we have learnt and practised for nearly two years.

For our special benefit, our hostess provides us with frog-pie. But I only learn that later in the evening. It tastes like chicken pie. They are not ordinary frogs, gathered in the fields, but specially reared animals. They have been carefully fed and fattened. Only the limbs appear to have been used. It is an excellent dish and we enjoy it immensely. The wine is easily the best we have ever had: it sparkles, and has 'body' in it. Our table napkins are spotless. We had forgotten all about such things in the mud of Flanders, and on the Somme battlefields.

After dinner we have music and cigars and coffee. We lounge in comfortable chairs and forget all about our troubles. The hours pass by, and we cannot remember spending a happier evening. Before we leave for the camp, we promise to go to dinner three times a week with our friends. They are the quintessence of hospitality, and wish to do everything to make us happy while we are among them.

Each day we do a little light fatigue duty. Two hours each morning is the time for the first week. As we gain strength, the time is increased. We peel potatoes for our dinner, pick up matchsticks near the officers' quarters, clean out our huts, work in the quartermaster's stores, and make ourselves useful in a score of ways. Then we pass on to light physical training and a little Company drill. We have daily lectures on the parts of a rifle, and the stoppages of a Lewis gun, how to take cover in action, the long and the short jab with a bayonet, and the necessity for the care of our feet in the trenches.

We are taken out for short route marches. We go along the country lanes and look upon the same fair fields of France as did Henry V of England in the fifteenth century. But the times have changed. He plundered and laid waste the very things which we endeavour to preserve. *Autres temps, autres moeurs.*

Each day a draft leaves for the Front. I notify my French friends that in three days I shall be going back to the line, and shall not be able to see them again before my departure.

My eyes have by no means recovered. The slightest breeze or bright light causes them to become filled with tears. But when you are marked fit, you are fit, no matter how you feel or what you say.

CHAPTER FOURTEEN

Almost Back into the Cauldron

We line up in front of the office in answer to a bugle. It is four o'clock in the afternoon. There are about a hundred and fifty of us all told, and we look resplendent in our new uniforms. Rifles and equipment have been handed out to us, and we are made ready for the trenches once more. Two or three officers pass hurriedly along in front of us. We are being inspected, but it is purely a formal arrangement. In less than five minutes the inspection is over. The officers just walk past without looking at us. Perhaps we have just interrupted a hand of Bridge, and they want to get back to their game.

We form fours, turn to the right and march out of the camp. Even the poorest and meanest of us have a bit of a pageant going towards the grave. A bugle band goes in front of us, to give a little dignity to the occasion. The buglers strut along as though the winning of the war depended upon their mock heroics.

The procession is not of our seeking. We should prefer to find our own way to the station and to get into the carriages like ordinary people. A lieutenant and two subalterns are in charge of our party. They have probably conducted hundreds of such drafts to the station. A few men turn out to see us off and to wave us farewell. They know that their time of departure will not be long delayed.

Soon after we leave the convalescent camp, the band ceases to play. We swing along down the road, making for the town which is about three miles distant. As we reach the outskirts of the town the band blares forth once more and we march at attention. The civilians scarcely look at us as we go along the street. They have become accustomed to drafts leaving for the Front, as it is a daily occurrence.

On the pavement, outside the station, my French friends are waiting for me. They have come to see me off. While we wait for the train, I fall out of the ranks and talk to them. Their kindness is unbounded.

They have brought me a large hamper of good things, and ask me to share them with the other men in my compartment. It is wonderful how they have been able to collect so much food. There is a cold roast fowl, bread, biscuits, wine, fruit, cigars and other things which I had thought were unprocurable. We talk for twenty minutes and then I climb into the carriage. They wish me good luck, and stand waving their handkerchiefs until the train disappears round the bend.

These people are altogether different from the French peasants who live nearer the trenches. Perhaps they are more well-to-do, and therefore have enough and to spare. Or their losses may not have been so great as those of the people whose homes have been destroyed. In Belgium and Flanders the farm-wives took the handles off their pumps, so that we could not even get water to wash the mud of the trenches from our faces. It is good to know that there are some people who look upon us as friends rather than thieves.

The twilight fades, and as darkness comes we settle down in our carriage to enjoy the evening meal. We do not finish until all the food has gone. Over the cigars we exchange stories and reminiscences. One of our party is able to throw a new light upon the war. He asks us if we are aware that the English Government pays rent to the French Government for the land which is occupied by British troops. From the sea to the Somme, the land is hired out, and thousands of pounds are paid monthly. We are staggered. War economics is an entirely different thing from peace economics.

We cannot understand such an arrangement. Soldiers from every corner of the British Empire have flocked to check the German advance into France, and have died by the score of thousand to do so. When they succeed in holding the enemy, a retaining fee is demanded for the ground which they occupy. This would explain the fact that for a long time our pay was sixpence a day, and only after much agitation was it raised to a shilling and then to a shilling and sixpence a day. There is not enough money to go all round, and he who is farthest from home fares the worst. It is ever thus in life.

I am reminded of a case that came to my notice in England. While training, I had the good fortune to be befriended by a kindly old gentleman who asked me to visit him at his home. One evening, just before I left for the Front, he asked me if it could possibly be true that the infantryman was paid at the rate of sixpence a day. I assured him that such was the case. He then asked me how it was possible to manage on such pay. We went on talking, and finally he told me about himself. He had retired some years before the war began. Then the authorities discovered that he knew something about pigs, and he was asked to buy pigs for the Government. He was supplied with a first-class railway warrant, and with salary and commission, he never received less than twenty pounds a week. Without in any way wishing to be disrespectful to the old gentleman, we conclude that everyone who buys pigs to feed the troops is of as much value as well over a hundred foot soldiers.

The train rattles along, and one by one we fall asleep. The last one awake puts out the light.

All the next day we swing along on the narrow gauge railway. Men race along the track to get hot water from the engine. They get back into their carriages as they come alongside. We drink tea at intervals, and eat the sandwiches with which we have been provided. We play cards, sleep, tell stories and read a little to pass the time.

A second night passes, and in the early morning we enter the battle area. There is no sign of any living thing for many miles. Villages and scattered homesteads lie in ruins. We reflect that someone once loved these places, and patiently piled brick upon brick to make a home for women and little children. Later, they became strong points, and served as jumping-off places for an attack, or as something to be defended to the last man.

It is a wet morning. There are pools of water lying everywhere. There is nothing on earth more utterly desolate than the old Somme battlefields when rain has fallen – unless it is the much-hated and dreaded Ypres Salient.

The train comes to a halt and we get out. There is scarcely anything to indicate that we have arrived at a station, other than the name which has been knocked about by shell-fire and heavy bombs. Only the ruins remain.

We line up in the road, and pull the collars of our greatcoats up to our ears. It is an hour before we move off. In the army there is always somebody or something to wait for. Then we move off to an obscure little village eight kilometres away. Before we reach there we are all soaked to the skin. All the billets are occupied.

Not a single house remains intact. Sandbags filled with earth are used to stop holes and to buttress up the walls. Troops occupy every hole and corner where they can find shelter from the driving wind and rain. Little wisps of smoke curl upwards where the Tommies struggle hard to make themselves some tea.

We move about in search of a resting place, but can find nothing better than a cow byre. Only two walls remain standing. A number of soldiers huddle themselves close to them. The floor of the shed is sloping to allow for drainage, and as I am almost the last man in I come off badly. The concrete floor is littered with straw. But the straw is soaking wet and the continuous rain keeps it wet. I decide to go no further, but throw down my equipment and book a place.

Before it is dark we all go to bed, otherwise we should not see where the men are lying. The rain continues throughout the night, but I pull my overcoat over my head, and do not notice the discomfort. I wake up several times, but the march has made me tired and I soon drop off to sleep again.

In the morning I cannot move. I can scarcely breathe. Hot flushes come over me, and I feel faint when I try to rise. In my side there is a stabbing pain, and it shoots through me like forked lightning when I take a deep breath. It is as though someone pushed a red-hot bayonet into me. I think of the Jerry whom the Aussies ripped open with their foot-long bayonets at the end of their rifles. He saw them coming at him, and must have died many times before his death.

The bugle blows for breakfast. I am hungry, but do not want any food. The others come back to the cow byre with their rations of hot tea, bread, porridge and bacon. One of them picks up my mess tin and volunteers to fetch my breakfast. I tell him he can have everything but the tea.

I am propped up against the wall, and sip tea out of the billy can. It does me no good. I have been wet through a hundred times before and suffered no ill consequences, but this time it is different. Perhaps it is because my health has been undermined. I breathe in short gasps and my pulse races. When by any chance I take a long breath unthinkingly, a stab of pain causes me to squirm, and my face betrays the agony.

After breakfast comes the sick parade. Two men help me along to the hut of the Medical Officer. I hardly know whether I am fortunate or unfortunate. Ten miles away my Battalion is in rest billets: I hear that it is about to go into action again.

The doctor is busy and cannot see me for some time. I sit on a stone outside his hut and lean back against a wall. There are several wounded cases awaiting attention, as well as a number of men who have reported sick. A heavy drizzle is falling, the road runs with mud and slush.

When my turn comes, an orderly helps me into the surgery. The doctor is a young man and asks me a few questions. He presses with his hands here and there, and tells me to take a long, deep breath. My temperature is taken, and in five minutes he has finished with me. He says that I have pleurisy. The sergeant clerk makes out my ticket and fastens it to a button on my tunic. Thermogene is wound round my thorax, and I am made ready to be sent down the line again.

In the afternoon the motor ambulances take the sick and wounded to the rear. I am carried into a car and we do not stop until we arrive at a Casualty Clearing Station. As usual, it is full of troops. Nurses and orderlies are almost falling over each other; there are so many of them needed to look after the troops.

Again I am examined. The doctor says that I have dry pleurisy. He gives me an injection and tells me to avoid breathing deeply. The advice is not necessary, but it is kindly meant. I find it best to take in half-breaths. When I forget to do so, my side seems to become alive and flaming. The pain subsides again, and I inwardly register a resolve to forget no more – to breathe only in short gasps.

The clean bed smells sweet. The sheets are snow-white, and I comfort myself with the thought that it is far better to be ill in hospital than to go once more into the mud and blood of the trenches.

In time, I am able to be moved, and make way for the wounded who come down the line every day. Our hospital train is full but no-one knows our destination. In two days we reach the Base, and a fleet of cars takes us to different hospitals. I find myself back in the hospital which I was previously in, but in a different ward.

The days go past slowly. But when I am able to sit up, I write and tell my French friends that I am once more in their midst. A few days later I receive a very charming letter from them. The following Sunday, the family comes to visit me as before. They bring certain delicacies which they think I may be able to eat, and they express their joy at seeing me again. One feels that it is almost worth being ill, so warm is their welcome.

During my convalescence, I walk about the hospital grounds. German prisoners do all the fatigue work, and they appear to have the run of the place. They are not shadowed everywhere, but move about freely. Our men are not unkind to them. As they carry coal into the wards, the Tommies tell them to stand beside the stoves and warm themselves. They give them cigarettes, chocolate, writing paper and a handful of tobacco. The prisoners are young boys and middle-aged men. One strapping fellow, about forty years of age, interests me, and I resolve to seek him out. He reminds me of the first man I deliberately shot during an attack upon the enemy. They might easily be brothers. I feel the prick of conscience, and resolve to do what I can to make prison life a little more bearable for him than it would otherwise be. I feel sorry for him and also for myself. Our positions might easily have been reversed.

One day, I follow him to the coal yard and try to talk to him. He cannot speak a word of English and I do not understand his language. But there is one thing which we both understand, and that is that neither of us feels any hostility for the other. I give him cigarettes, tobacco and matches. In exchange, he gives me a leather wallet. In it he keeps photographs and letters. He shows me the photos of his wife and three little children. I do not need to be told who they are. More than ever I feel sorry for the prisoner, and I wonder if the man whom I shot carried such things in his pocket book. There was no time to rifle his pockets. But probably some German peasant woman has been doomed to a lifetime struggle to bring up her children unaided by a man.

But it was not possible to do otherwise in action. The victory goes to him who gets his shot in first, and though one feels no sense of enmity towards a man because he is dressed in a uniform of a different colour, yet one knows the consequences of being slow in the field.

A few days later, the prisoner brings me a photo frame. He has made it in his spare time, from a piece of wood he has picked up in the camp. It is large enough to hold a postcard, and is carved at the bottom. It has very little value, but it has taken hours to make. Its chief value lies in the fact that it has kept the maker occupied for several hours, and given him something to think about and to do. It has prevented him thinking all the time about his beloved Germany and his little family who are waiting for his return. He is like a wild bird in a cage, in some respects. He longs for his freedom, and eats his heart out in captivity. But he knows that the war will soon end, and that he will get home again, no matter who wins or who loses. The chief thing for him to do is to keep occupied in the meantime, and not to think too much about himself. It is the surest way of being restored to his family.

Every few days he brings a number of photo frames into the hut. They are of different sizes and prices and designs. Nearly all the wounded soldiers buy them, especially those who know that they have finished with the war. They will do to take home as souvenirs, or to distribute among one's friends.

Every day fresh casualties are brought into the hospital. The beds are kept full, and certain wards are set apart for the wounded prisoners. We hear and read about fresh American divisions being thrown into the line, and the German retreat. But from the numbers of troops that come down to the Base hospitals, the enemy might be making a stiff resistance. His machine-gunners fire into the masses of advancing soldiers, and mow them down in swathes. Then the gunners themselves are caught, and no one spares them. The losses on both sides are enormous. But there is no doubt that the end is drawing near. The last desperate throw of the Jerries cannot hold up for long the advance of the Allies. It is simply a question of time.

In the hospital there are rumours that an armistice will soon be signed. But most of us discredit such rumours. We recall the occasions when we were supposed to be relieved, and no relief came. We recall the night operations and the forced marches, when acting as a flying column, when it had been rumoured that the plans had been altered. In brief, we have come to look upon all good news as something to buoy us up, and having no truth in reality. We have noticed for so long that a rumour is the method adopted in the Army to lessen fatigue and to give us fresh hope. It may be sound psychology, but when hope is too long deferred, we choose to live from moment to moment, and to take only what comes our way.

Before very long, we see references to an armistice in the newspapers. In the wards, long discussions take place every day. A few weeks ago, the possibility of an armistice seemed so remote that none of us even gave any thought to the matter. At that time, the war would only end for us when we were all killed, and each side had insufficient troops left to carry on the war.

In our ward, most of us favour the cessation of hostilities. But there are some who think that the time has not yet come to end the war. Our troops have at last got moving, and each day the morale of the enemy becomes weaker. Even at the cost of further sacrifice, many men favour the continuation of the war until we enter the enemy's country. They would drive Jerry right back to the Rhine and treat his beautiful towns in the same way as the old mediaeval towns of Belgium and France have been treated. Their argument is based on sound common sense – that there is nothing like having things brought home to one.

Early in the morning we are warned that at eleven o'clock the armistice will be signed. We talk about what the troops will be doing at the Front, and most of us agree that it would not be worth running any risk during the last few hours. Some of the more blood-thirsty ones, and many who have spent most of their soldiering days at the Base declare that they would have a last parting shot at the enemy before the 'Cease fire' sounds.

We play cards and smoke cigarettes till eleven o'clock draws nigh. Then, from across the river we hear a siren. The ships in the harbour at Le Havre and in the river all take up the signal, and from the town three miles away, we hear the roar of the citizens and soldiers. This tells us that the war is over. We cannot understand it. It is too big a matter for us to comprehend. We have become accustomed to soldiering, and it is not possible for us to realise that we have finished with uniforms and forming fours and ceremonial parades and going over the top to attack the enemy and drive him out of his strong points. We only know that the war is over and that we still live.

All the morning we hear noises from the town. When dinner time is finished, the roads become blocked with soldiers. They all stream down the hill into the town. Everybody who is able to walk goes down to join in the celebrations. The hospitals and convalescent camps lose three-quarters of their patients. Only those who cannot leave their beds remain behind. France is en fête, and patients in blue hospital clothes hurry down the hill.

We enter the town by way of the main street. There are no signs of the military police. They probably know that this is the soldiers' day and that it would not be safe for them to attend to their work. All the streets are thronged with people. Civilians and soldiers jostle each other and call to one another in familiar terms. The estaminets are all thrown open, and free drinks are given to anybody who wants them. Here and there a soldier staggers along the pavement, supported by one or two of his comrades. Occasionally, a man falls down in the middle of the street. An ambulance car picks him up and takes him away. Officers and men all behave alike. They enter the estaminets together and leave together. They link arms and go along the streets singing the British Army songs. Military discipline is forgotten for one evening; nobody exercises any control over anyone else. Whatever their relationship in the past, all are resolved to give themselves up to the joys of the present.

A company of Poilus strike up 'The Marseillaise', but their efforts are soon drowned by 'Blighty', 'Tipperary', 'Armentières', and other songs to which the British troops have marched for over four long years. By the time the clocks strike midnight, the streets become less crowded. We make our way back to the hospital, and do not trouble to find a way in through the hedges or fences. It is nearly three o'clock in the morning, and the sentry stands at the main gate with rifle in hand. But he does not challenge us as we pass. The Guard Room would be useless on Armistice night.

We go to our ward, but there is no sleep in us. Every hut in the hospital is lit up with electric light, and the stoves are piled high with coal. We sit about and drink French wines. There appears to be no end to the supply. As soon as one bottle is emptied, another takes its place. The supplies of the estaminets have been much depleted.

When daylight breaks, we go to our beds. In a few minutes most of us are asleep. We live. The war is over.

Epilogue

The years passed. In 1931, a number of men were gathered together in the house in which Toc H was born in South Africa. This was at a place called St Matthew's. One of those present was a German pastor. He was Pastor Schantz of the Lutheran Church in Keiskama Hoek, an attractive village five miles from St. Matthew's. Another of those present was an English schoolmaster.

The German pastor was a very good looking man. He was highly intelligent, and he spoke English fluently. He looked to be about forty-five years of age.

During the evening, the German pastor and the English schoolmaster talked to one another. They talked about the war.

'I suppose that you were too young to have seen anything of the war,' said Pastor Schantz to me.

'I was young,' I replied, 'but I served on the Western Front.'

'I served mostly in Salonika,' said he, 'but I was on the Arras part of the line in France for a while in the late summer of 1918. I was there when the big English attack took place in the Second Battle of Arras.'

'Where exactly were you?' I asked.

'In a trench in front of Vis-en-Artois', he replied.

'I was one of those who drove you out of it and chased you for some distance. You were very fortunate to have got away. Many of your friends were not so lucky. They stayed behind for ever,' I said.

'We meet here to-night under very different circumstances,' said Pastor Schantz. 'The last time was six thousand miles away.'

'And thirteen years ago. And truth is certainly stranger than fiction,' I replied.